Russia and the Iranian Nuclear Program:
Replay or Breakthrough?

Russia and the Iranian Nuclear Program: Replay or Breakthrough?

By John W. Parker

Institute for National Strategic Studies
Strategic Perspectives, No. 9

Series Editors: Nicholas Rostow and Phillip C. Saunders

National Defense University Press
Washington, D.C.
March 2012

First printing, March 2012

For current publications of the Institute for National Strategic Studies, please go to the National Defense University Web site at: www.ndu.edu/inss.

Contents

Executive Summary

Despite protests across Russia sparked by last December's fraud-filled Duma (parliament) elections, Vladimir Putin is preparing to return to the presidency this May. Will Putin replay his 2004–2008 approach to Iran, during which Russia negotiated the S–300 air defense system contract with Tehran? Or will he continue Russia's breakthrough in finding common ground with the United States on Iran seen under President Dmitriy Medvedev, who tore up the S–300 contract?

While coordinating more closely with Washington on Iran during the Medvedev administration, Moscow did not and has not closed the door to engagement with Tehran. In 2010, Russia voted for new, enhanced sanctions against Iran at the United Nations Security Council (UNSC). Nevertheless, Moscow and Tehran have remained engaged diplomatically, and their relations have stabilized and begun to recover from their winter 2010–2011 low point.

At the same time, Russia continues to insist that Iran comply with its commitments under the Nuclear Non-Proliferation Treaty (NPT) and cooperate fully with International Atomic Energy Agency (IAEA) inspectors. However, Russia is wary of pushing so hard on compliance lest Iran entirely abandon its treaty obligations and walk out of the NPT.

In February 2011, Moscow began to oppose another round of UNSC sanctions, and in July 2011 put forward a "step-by-step" initiative coordinated with other Permanent Members of the Security Council and Germany (the so-called P5+1). The Moscow approach offered Tehran a gradual reduction in sanctions in return for improved cooperation with the IAEA in monitoring Iran's nuclear enrichment program.

Putin's resentment of U.S. power and suspicion of American motives will make for frostier atmospherics between Moscow and Washington. Nonetheless, mistrust of Iran will continue to outweigh Putin's misgivings about the United States. Everything else being equal, the United States will always be more important to Russia than Iran.

Most Russian experts now believe that Iran is advancing toward a military nuclear weapons program—though it has not made a final decision to go all the way—and a ballistic missile program to accompany it. Russia sees these programs as a threat to its interests.

Moscow's decision to toughen its approach to Iran on the nuclear issue is likely to remain the basis of Russian policy in the period ahead, so long as the U.S.-Russia "reset" does not totally collapse, especially if Iran does not move toward greater cooperation with the IAEA. Russia's looming domestic and external challenges will strengthen the inclination to continue some variant of reset, even if through Putin's clenched teeth.

Russian experts warn that a serious fraying in U.S.-Russia relations might cause Moscow to tilt back toward Tehran. The record on the S–300 contract, however, suggests that any rollback in Russian support for sanctions will depend mostly on whether Iran decides to cooperate more fully with the IAEA in clarifying Iran's nuclear enrichment program and moving toward verifiable restraints on its enrichment activities.

On regional issues, however, Russia and Iran will continue at least to appear to pursue neighborly engagement with each other. The Arab Spring has pushed forward overlapping but not identical challenges and opportunities to the positions of both countries in the Middle East, including how to deal with Syria. The impending American withdrawal from Afghanistan has raised the prospect that Russia and Iran may once again have to partner closely in resisting Taliban threats to their regional equities, as they did before 9/11.

Engagement has historically been Moscow's default setting for dealing with Tehran. Russia's current step-by-step initiative appears designed to continue engagement, while underscoring Russia's potential role as a mediator between Iran and the international community. From Moscow's perspective, Iran's withdrawal from the NPT would be dangerous and the world community should do everything to keep Iran in the NPT and IAEA inspectors in Iran, even if under less than ideal circumstances. At the same time, step-by-step does not lessen UNSC pressure on Iran unless Tehran improves cooperation with the IAEA.

Iran's collaboration with the IAEA is therefore crucially important for the future of Russian-Iranian relations. Their tone and tint will depend on Iran's willingness or unwillingness to improve its situation with respect to the IAEA and UNSC. If Iran's relations with the IAEA improve, the prospect of new Russian-Iranian contracts and other cooperation improves.

Moscow's approach to Tehran will always differ from Washington's, even when Russian and American policies coincide on some major points with respect to Iran (as they do now). Moscow does not want to provoke Iranian meddling in Central Asia, the South Caucasus, or Russian North Caucasus. At the same time, Tehran is careful not to cross any Russian "red lines" in these areas.

Russia's and Iran's shared security interests include preventing any outside military attack against Iran. Russian diplomacy has tried to avoid this outcome over the years even as it has also sought to discourage Iran from pursuing its nuclear enrichment program. Moscow's effort to discourage the use of force against Iran is guided by the fear that any foreign military action against nearby Iran would have spillover effects that would directly affect Russian security interests in ways difficult to predict and contain.

This paper is based on information that was current as of January 9, 2012.

Introduction

Russian-Iranian relations over the centuries and in recent decades have been complex and elastic. They have been simultaneously good in some areas while bad in others. Even at their worst, they have been able to stretch without breaking. A visitor to the Kremlin Armory can admire the 89-carat diamond that the Shah of Persia sent to Nicholas I to assuage the murder by a Tehran mob in 1829 of Russian Ambassador Alexander Griboyedov and his staff. The spectacular gift was part of a package deal to which both sides contributed to put the ugly incident behind them.[1] More recently, Moscow greatly angered Tehran in 2010 when it broke the contract for the S–300 (U.S./North Atlantic Treaty Organization [NATO]–designated SA–20) long-range air defense missile system, yet the two countries have subsequently worked hard for a semblance of continued engagement. (See boxes "The S–300 Contract" for the rise and fall of the S–300 contract.)

In December 2007, Iranian Defense Minister Mohammad Najjar revealed the contract during a visit to Moscow when he told the press that "S–300 air defense systems will be supplied to Iran within the framework of an agreement earlier concluded with Russia."[2] Russian experts immediately predicted that the sale of the S–300 to Iran would create new tensions between Washington and Moscow.[3] Washington had earlier objected to Russia's sale of the short-range Tor-M1 air defense system to Iran.[4] Now, the day after the S–300 announcement, the Russian press reported White House spokesman Scott Stanzel's declaration of U.S. "concern" over the prospective sale of the S–300, which was described as a sign of Washington's extreme irritation.[5]

There may have been no connection between nondelivery of the S–300 during President Bush's last year in office and Washington's clear opposition to the deal. After all, Moscow's relations with the Bush administration had begun to deteriorate in 2003 when the United States invaded Iraq despite Russian objections. These ties became worse when Moscow saw Washington behind the "color revolutions" of 2003–2005 in Georgia, Ukraine, and Kyrgyzstan, and when Washington subsequently encouraged Tbilisi and Kyiv to pursue NATO membership. They then went into the deep-freezer after the August 2008 Russia-Georgia war and Washington's announcement the same month of plans for a new missile defense system in Europe.[6]

Najjar's successor, Brigadier General Ahmad Vahidi, would later claim that Russia should have delivered the S–300 systems to Iran in summer 2008.[7] If Moscow in 2008 was indeed already holding up transfer of the S–300 to Iran, it may have begun to suffer from seller's remorse. If so, it could have been waiting to see the outcomes of presidential elections in the United States in November 2008 and in Iran in June 2009 before deciding whether to go ahead with the contracted

The S–300 System: Why So Important?

On December 5, 2005, Russian Defense Minister Sergei Ivanov confirmed news reports that Moscow at the end of November had signed a contract to deliver about 30 short-range Tor-M1 surface-to-air missile systems in the next 2 years. Ivanov described the Tor-M1 as "an exclusively 100 percent defensive weapon." The system was the crown jewel in a package of new contracts reportedly worth more than $1 billion, including an accord to modernize Iranian air force equipment and to supply patrol craft for the Iranian navy.[1]

The Tor-M1 was described as capable of identifying up to 48 targets and simultaneously firing at 2 of them within a 12-kilometer range at altitudes up to 6 kilometers.[2] Speculation was rife that Iran would use the system to protect nuclear installations such as the Bushehr nuclear power plant.

However, on its own, the Tor-M1 system could not provide much comfort to the guardians of Iran's nuclear facilities. As analyst Pavel Felgenhauer pointed out, the relatively short-range Tor-M1s could not defend hardened nuclear sites against blockbuster munitions released from high-flying bombers. The system could do so effectively only if linked to the much more sophisticated long-range S–300 air defense missile system, which Iran reportedly was also seeking to acquire.[3]

When Iranian Defense Minister Najjar announced in December 2007 that Iran had finalized a contract with Russia for future delivery of the S–300, the Russian press asserted that the system could strike targets at altitudes up to 27 kilometers from as far away as 150 kilometers. With the S–300, Tehran would finally have an echeloned air defense capable of protecting sites such as Bushehr and Natanz from an extensive array of air attacks.

Possession of the S–300 would enhance Iran's confidence that it could complicate any U.S. or Israeli attack plans, and would degrade any would be attacker's chances of success in a campaign to destroy Iran's noncivilian nuclear facilities. After the announcement, the Russian press noted great concern in the Israeli press over the potential of the S–300 to make Iran invulnerable to air strikes by the United States or Israel.[4]

[1] "Russia to Supply Missile Systems to Iran," *Agentstvo Voyennykh Novostey*, December 2, 2005, CEP20051202027065 (Open Source Center product number).

[2] Aleksandr Babakin and Vladimir Ivanov, "Bombshell for Greater Middle East? Delivery of Surface-to-Air Missile Systems to Iran Threatens to Have Explosive Consequences," *Nezavisimoye Voyennoye Obozreniye*, December 9, 2005, CEP20051209436002; Konstantin Lantratov and Alexandra Gritskova, "Iran Shields Its Nuclear Activities by Russian Missiles," *Kommersant.com*, December 26, 2007, CEP20071226950405; Yakovina Ivan and Ilya Kramnik, "Superiority Complex. Russia Prepared to Give Iran the Chance Not to Be Intimidated by United States," *Lenta.ru*, December 27, 2007, CEP20071228358004; and Pavel Felgenhauer, "Iran Takes Delivery of Russian Tor-M1 Missiles," Jamestown Foundation, *Eurasia Daily Monitor* 4, no. 12, January 17, 2007, available at <www.jamestown.org/single/?no_cache=1&tx_ttnews%5Btt_news%5D=32397>.

[3] Felgenhauer.

[4] Felgenhauer; Ivan and Kramnik; Lantratov and Gritskova; and John W. Parker, *Persian Dreams: Moscow and Tehran Since the Fall of the Shah* (Washington, DC: Potomac Books, Inc., 2009), 260, 302–303, 309.

deliveries. However, there were a number of alternative explanations, including technical problems. But a Russian source who claimed involvement in the negotiations later attributed the delay to drawn-out Iranian haggling over the price of the contract.[8]

In any event, Russian-Iranian relations stalled in 2008–2009 over Iran's nonresponsiveness to the updated P5+1 (the Permanent Members of the Security Council and Germany) incentives package of June 2008.[9] Even earlier, Moscow had been put off by Tehran's brush-off of what seemed to have been a Russian face-saving compromise offer. First broached in November 2005, the proposed joint-venture to enrich uranium for Iran temporarily—on Russian territory under international control without turning over to Iran any hands-on technical control of the enrichment phase—would have staved off referral of the issue to the United Nations Security Council (UNSC).[10]

Nevertheless, Moscow in 2008 continued to play up its contacts with Tehran in part to underscore Russia's pique with Washington, but was frustrated with Tehran's unwillingness to come clean with the International Atomic Energy Agency (IAEA) on Iran's nuclear program and Tehran's defiance of the UNSC resolutions. Over the years, Russia had tempered international pressure on Iran. At the same time, Russia had approved numerous IAEA reports critical of Tehran and had voted for a series of Security Council resolutions imposing or upholding sanctions. In September 2008, while blocking efforts to extend earlier sanctions, Russia nevertheless kept pressure on Iran by voting for the fifth UNSC sanctions resolution since 2006.[11]

In late 2008, even before Barack Obama's inauguration, hints began to surface that Moscow was rethinking the S–300 deal and perhaps moving toward holding up the transfer of the missiles.[12] Suggestions of shifting ground between Moscow, Tehran, and Washington began to crop up after President-elect Obama suggested in December on *Meet the Press* that a "reset" was needed in U.S.-Russia ties.[13] By February 4, 2009, Rosoboroneksport General Director Anatoliy Isaykin stated publicly that the S–300 contract still needed presidential approval for the system's transfer to Iran to be executed.[14]

Against this background of Moscow's already shifting relations with Tehran and Washington, the rise of the Green Movement to protest President Mahmoud Ahmadinejad's fraud-filled reelection on June 12, 2009, set in motion dramatic developments within Iran. They soon began to affect Tehran's decisionmaking on the nuclear issue and Russia's—and the world's—response. By the end of 2009, they created deep rifts within the Iranian elite, the estrangement of a significant sector of the Iranian urban public from the Islamic regime, and speculation that the wave of protests might succeed in removing Ahmadinejad from office before the end of his second term and perhaps even lead to revolutionary regime change.

Much to Moscow's chagrin, it got sucked up into the intra-Iranian contretemps that those elections provoked. Ahmadinejad's first trip abroad after his June 12 "victory" was to Yekaterinburg, Russia, for a summit of the Shanghai Cooperation Organization (SCO), in which Iran has observer status.[15] He arrived a day late because of clashes, described as the worst rioting in Tehran in years, that had broken out over protests of the official election results. Nevertheless, as polite hosts, Russian President Dmitriy Medvedev and the other heads of state present in Yekaterinburg congratulated Ahmadinejad on his reelection. But the Russian and Iranian leaders held only a truncated bilateral meeting on the margins of the SCO summit, after which Medvedev was to be host of the first summit of the BRIC (Brazil, Russia, India, and China) countries.[16]

Russian Deputy Foreign Minister Sergei Ryabkov told the press that "Elections in Iran are an internal affair of the Iranian people, but we welcome the newly elected president of that state." Ryabkov said that Ahmadinejad's trip to Russia was "a signal of successful mutual relations in the future."[17] However, Russia was soon forced to shift its line as Tehran dealt violently with mounting protests. On June 20, a video captured the final moments of a young woman named Neda Agha-Soltan as she bled to death on a Tehran side street after being shot not far from antigovernment protests.[18] After the shocking video circulated around the world, Foreign Minister Sergey Lavrov continued to insist that the election and its aftermath were Iran's own internal affair. However, he now added that "Naturally, we express our most serious concern over the use of force and the death of peaceful citizens."[19]

Russia's attempt to straddle the fence helped provoke "Death to Russia" slogans on July 17 when Ahmadinejad rival and former President Ali Akbar Hashemi Rafsanjani spoke to tens of thousands gathered in and around Tehran University's main prayer hall. The vast crowd included main opposition candidate Mir Hussein Mousavi.[20] According to commentators, Green Movement hostility to Russia was based on the perception that Russia supported the Iranian regime as well as a desire to flout the government's routine anti-Americanism.[21]

As Green Movement demonstrations continued in the streets after July 17, reformers and moderates inside the regime unleashed a wave of criticism of Ahmadinejad's diplomatic reliance on Russia and China, a policy known as "Look East." They did not show any gratitude to Russia and China for having tempered international sanctions. Instead, they castigated Russia especially for not having done more to shelter Iran's nuclear program, which these Iranian moderates defended rather than criticized.[22] It was a taste of more to come.

In Russia, there was criticism of relying on Ahmadinejad and some calls for reaching out to Iranian moderates, among whom Russian reports implied Mousavi and Rafsanjani belonged. An editorial in *Nezavisimaya Gazeta*, for example, asserted that "The notion that Iran is a regional power that Russia would be able to use as a trump card in its relations with the West has proved to be mistaken." More to the point, it continued, "Actually putting money on personal relations with Ahmadinejad appears counterproductive." Instead, it mused, the Russian and Iranian publics would be better served if Moscow developed contacts with "more moderate forces" in Iran and there were increased international pressure on the Tehran regime. It concluded that "Recent events in the republic, when Ahmadinejad's opponents shouted 'Death to Russia!' slogans, would appear to indicate that among a considerable section of the Iranian population Moscow's advocacy in defense of Ahmadinejad's government has not met with approval."[23]

Unfortunately for Moscow, moderates with influence in Tehran became harder and harder to find. To be sure, large-scale demonstrations, accompanied by widely publicized regime violence against protestors, continued into the fall and winter of 2009. Demonstrators in Tehran reportedly planned to attack the Russian embassy on the 30th anniversary of the November 4, 1979, takeover of the American Embassy.[24] During antigovernment demonstrations on February 11, 2010, the 31st anniversary of the Islamic revolution, there were again chants of "Death to Russia."[25] But by the end of the winter, Iran's moderates were intimidated, fragmented, and marginalized.[26]

Even in the event of a comeback, however, regime moderates and the Green Movement were now predisposed against Russia because of its apparent backing of Ahmadinejad. Moreover, hardliners increasingly had little use for Russia because of its failure to come through with decisive support against American pressure in the UN Security Council.

In Moscow, Yelena Dunaeva of the Oriental Studies Institute closely tracked Iranian opinion toward Russia. She reported that Internet polling in fall 2009 had found that 95 percent of Iranian respondents held anti-Russian opinions. This percentage had increased since spring 2009 as U.S.-Russia relations warmed up and Russia continued to push back the completion date of the Bushehr nuclear power plant, where work had been under way since 1995; public opinion attributed the delays in finishing the plant to Russia yielding to pressure from the United States. In June 2009, noted Dunaeva, pro-regime media in Tehran played up Medvedev's meeting with Ahmadinejad in Yekaterinburg 3 days after his disputed election. The reformist camp, however, saw the meeting as Russia's endorsement of the strong-arm tactics used by the regime against demonstrators demanding a recount of the election results.[27]

The S–300 Contract: Inconclusive Early Years

One of the earliest mentions of a possible sale of the S–300 to Iran came during the April 1997 visit to Moscow of Majles Speaker Nateq-Nuri. This was right after the January 1997 contract to sell S–300s to Cyprus and just as Russian-Iranian cooperation in bringing peace to Tajikistan was nearing fruition. This placed it squarely at the high-point of warming Russian-Iranian relations following Foreign Minister Yevgeniy Primakov's visit to Tehran in December 1996.[1]

Russian commentary at the time described the possible sale of the S–300 to Iran as a potential riposte to another wave of NATO expansion eastward. Then First Deputy Premier Anatoly Chubays told Deputy Secretary of State Strobe Talbott that "hard-liners were exploiting resentment over NATO expansion in their advocacy of 'a strategic marriage of convenience with Iran.'"[2]

The S–300 popped up on Iran's own Russian shopping list as far back as 1998,[3] most likely in connection with Foreign Minister Kamal Kharrazi's visit to Moscow late that February.[4]

However, the timing of the Iranian request was not auspicious. The S–300 contract that Russia had signed with Cyprus was already in trouble; moreover, the Iranian request got buffeted by competing views in Moscow on selling sensitive weapons to Iran. Signs of the time were Prime Minister Viktor Chernomyrdin's issuance of the "catchall" Directive No. 57 export control instruction on January 22, 1998, and the beginning of publicity given to arrests in Moscow of Iranian dual-use purchasers. The atmosphere would soon get worse with Iran's first test launch of the Shahab-3 medium-range ballistic missile in July 1998, whose range meant that Iran could soon present a security threat to Russia itself.[5]

By December 29, 1998, the contract to sell S–300s to Cyprus had collapsed.[6] Threats to sell the S–300 to Iran died out in the Russian press. Moreover, this was the case despite Russia's dire economic condition following the collapse of the ruble that summer.

---

[1] John W. Parker, *Persian Dreams: Moscow and Tehran Since the Fall of the Shah* (Washington, DC: Potomac Books, Inc., 2009), 118–119; Igor Korotchenko, "Russian-Iranian Talks," *Nezavisimaya Gazeta*, April 11, 1997, FTS19970411000205; and Vyacheslav Zalomov, "West Declares Open Season on Iran," *Pravda Pyat*, April 12, 1997, FTS19970414000563.

[2] *Persian Dreams*, 120–121.

[3] Igor Korotchenko, "In Spite of U.S. Pressure," *Nezavisimoye Voyennoye Obozreniye*, September 21, 2001, CEP20010920000406.

[4] *Persian Dreams*, 144–145; ITAR–TASS, February 24, 1998, FTS19980224001327; and Interfax, February 25, 1998, FTS19980225000637.

[5] *Persian Dreams*, 119–127.

The S–300 Contract: Inconclusive Early Years (cont.)

[6] *Persian Dreams*, 145; and Sergey Gulyy, "No Prestige—Only Money," *Novyye Izvestiya*, December 31, 1998, FTS19981231000358. Republic of Cyprus President Glafkos Kliridhis officially announced the rejection of the S–300 contract and proposed the system be stationed on the Greek island of Crete instead of Cyprus.

Tehran Research Reactor Talks Do More Damage

Subsequently, political divisions among regime insiders checkmated what could be interpreted as an effort by Ahmadinejad to move toward a breakthrough with Washington and its P5+1 partners in talks on supplying fuel for the Tehran Research Reactor (TRR). Tehran's backtracking on a TRR deal in fall 2009 deflated the lingering perception in Moscow—and many other capitals—that it was still possible to do business with Iran's governing elite.

As Iran first agreed to but then backed off a deal to supply enriched uranium rods for the TRR, it further tried Moscow's—and others'—patience. Against the background of continuing domestic turmoil in Iran and revelations in late September 2009 of a secret enrichment plant at Fordow near Qom, Tehran raised international hopes, including Russian, but then dashed them.[28] Discovery of the Qom facility had prompted Medvedev to issue a special statement at the G-20 summit in Pittsburgh, Pennsylvania, in which he charged that Iran's failure to notify the IAEA for several years of the plant's construction was "a source of serious concern" and challenged Iran to prove its peaceful intentions. Looking ahead to the P5+1 meeting with Iran scheduled for October 1 to take up the TRR issue, Medvedev called on Iran to "take practical steps to restore trust to its nuclear program and ensure transparency."[29]

In Geneva on October 1, Iranian negotiators met with representatives of the P5+1. There they provisionally accepted a draft proposal developed through the IAEA to send as much as 1,200 kilograms, roughly the amount that Iran could otherwise use to produce its first nuclear weapon, to Russia for enrichment from 3.5 percent to the 20-percent level. The material would then be sent on to France for conversion to metal alloy fuel rods, which Iran did not have the facilities to produce. The rods would be used by the TRR to produce medical isotopes to treat some 850,000 kidney, heart, and cancer patients.

The 1,200 kilograms amounted to 75–80 percent of Iran's declared low enriched uranium stock, which had been estimated at 1,500 kilograms in July 2009 but had been growing at the rate of 80 kilograms per month since then. Since the rods could not be reconverted to weapons material, the deal would have put off the day when Iran would once again have enough enriched uranium stock to produce its first atomic weapon.

The negotiations and resulting deal were not conditioned on Iran's suspension of enrichment but at the same time did not explicitly recognize Iran's right to enrichment. Nevertheless, Tehran's acceptance of the deal would have postponed the day of reckoning over Iran's refusal to halt enrichment and perhaps even have set the stage for a more fundamental deal.[30] On October 21, this time meeting in Vienna, Iranian negotiators accepted the draft agreement, subject to government approval in Tehran.[31]

On October 29, in a speech broadcast live on state television, Ahmadinejad talked up the TRR deal. Although the Western powers had previously insisted on Iran's halting its nuclear enrichment program, they were now "ready for cooperation and participation on exchange of nuclear fuel and building power plants."[32] "We welcome cooperation on nuclear fuel, power plants and technology, and we are ready to cooperate," said the Iranian president.[33] According to Ahmadinejad, "Nuclear fuel supply for the Tehran reactor is an opportunity to evaluate the honesty of the powers and the [IAEA]."[34] Ahmadinejad boasted that no previous Iranian administration had been able to get a deal that in effect acknowledged Iran's right to continue enrichment. In fact, there was nothing in the TRR deal that indicated that the P5+1 would ever accept nuclear enrichment on Iranian territory. Nevertheless, it could be argued that the deal was a face-saving way for both sides to begin a discussion precisely on that point without requiring it as a precondition to further talks.[35]

Even as Ahmadinejad was speaking in favor of the TRR deal, however, Iran was beginning to walk away from it. Before long, it would in effect reject the arrangement by insisting that the swap take place on Iranian soil and on a piecemeal basis.[36] As Green Movement demonstrations continued to gather steam and spark intra-elite dissension, the Iranian president was being attacked from all sides of the political spectrum.[37] Instead of a breakthrough, the TRR initiative gave way to stalemate as Ahmadinejad was forced to retreat from his initial approval and as Supreme Leader Khamenei, who presumably had also initially consented to the TRR deal, also backpedaled.[38]

All of this led to further disenchantment in Moscow with Iran and uncertainty about what to do next. Whereas 2 to 3 years earlier, Moscow had seen both Washington and Tehran as part of the problem, it now saw the inability of the leadership in Tehran to reach out for a deal as the entire problem. Among observers in Moscow consulted by this author several months later, there was no expectation of improvement under Ahmadinejad, or that he would be succeeded by a more moderate figure in 2013. Even if the Green Movement somehow managed to replace the current regime, cautioned one, a more liberal regime would be even more in favor of acquiring a nuclear weapon. Several argued that there was a national consensus in favor of Iran becoming a nuclear power, which even pro-Shah Iranian exiles supported.[39]

Crunch Point: Resolution 1929

In the face of Iranian stalling, backtracking, and stonewalling on the nuclear issue and Moscow's increasing engagement with Washington on "reset," Russia continued to delay fulfillment of the S–300 contract. Ahmadinejad in response kicked off the first of several rounds of increasingly bitter accusations.

On November 27, 2009, Russia and China supported a tough IAEA Board of Governors statement. This criticized Iran for not suspending enrichment related activities as required by the Security Council and called on it immediately to suspend construction of the Qom facility.[40] Ahmadinejad responded on November 29 by stating that Iran would build 10 new enrichment plants.[41] On December 1, the Iranian president complained that "Russia made a mistake; Russia in my opinion does not have a proper understanding of the situation in the world today. Perhaps it went to the other side with inaccurate information."[42]

A few days after Ahmadinejad's statements, Russian national security expert Aleksey Arbatov said there had been a serious shift in Russian policy toward Iran. Russia now agreed in principle to "traumatizing" sanctions against Iran because "Iran has simply become conceited." The announcement of Iran's intention to build 10 more enrichment plants had "demonstrated to Russia that [Iran] not only does not value [Russian] support and its efforts for peaceful resolution of the problem, but that it simply does not care about its interests and obligations, does not care about the interests of nonproliferation."[43] According to Dmitri Trenin, director of the Carnegie Endowment's office in Moscow, Tehran's rejection of the TRR deal had persuaded Russians that Iran was up to no good on its nuclear program.[44]

On December 4, Tehran reinforced this view of Iran in Moscow when it said Iran would give the IAEA only 6 months notice before the announced new plants became operational, even though the IAEA position was that they had to be declared as soon as planning began.[45] Later the same month, on the margins of the UN Climate Change Conference in Copenhagen, Ahmadinejad gratuitously slapped Russia by stating that Iran planned to go to the UN to seek compensation for the damage done by the United States, Britain, and the Soviet Union on Iranian soil during World War II.[46] On February 7–8, 2010, Ahmadinejad ordered Iran's Atomic Energy Organization to commence enrichment to 20 percent at Natanz, in effect putting Iran much closer to possessing weapons-grade material and enough of it to produce a bomb.[47]

On March 1 in Paris, at a press conference with President Nicolas Sarkozy, Medvedev lamented that the situation with Iran was "unfortunately . . . deteriorating," that the international community's "exhortations . . . have yielded no results so far," and that Russia was willing to consider imposing sanctions if Iran failed to comply.[48] On March 6, Ahmadinejad gave Russian commercial pilots working in Iran 2 months to leave the country. Iranian commentary tied the decision to the crash of a Russian-piloted Iranian-leased Russian aircraft outside Mashhad, with 40 fatalities and reportedly due to pilot error. Russian experts, however, attributed the expulsion order to Iranian pique over Medvedev's comments in Paris.[49] In June, Iran would reportedly ban the use of Russian Tupolev Tu-154 planes in Iran.[50]

With China's agreement on March 24 to join in substantive talks on a new sanctions resolution, negotiations finally moved into high gear in the UN Security Council.[51] A month later, Medvedev told a Danish broadcaster that "So far Iran is not showing due understanding and acts quite irresponsibly. . . . Sanctions are a bad thing because they rarely bring any results. But when all other options have been exhausted, why not?"[52]

Meanwhile, Russia's stock in Tehran—never high in any event—continued to sag across the political spectrum. In early 2010, a high-level Russian veteran of direct dealings with Iran reportedly had found no closeness to Russia left at any level in Tehran. Instead, he had encountered a lot of contempt. The Iranians were not treating Russia as a major player, even though they recognized it as an independent one. However, in their view only the United States really counted.[53] By late April 2010, Dunaeva at the Oriental Institute surmised that in Tehran leadership circles the majority still remained optimistic about the prospects for a strategic alliance between Russia and Iran. However, she warned, the ranks of pessimists calling for caution and distrust toward Russia had grown, and could eventually lead to unforeseeable changes in Iranian policy toward Russia.[54]

Indeed, relations soon sharply worsened. When Brazilian President Luiz Inácio Lula da Silva stopped in Moscow on May 14 and conferred with Medvedev on a proposed initiative by Brazil and Turkey to revisit the TRR deal with Ahmadinejad, the Russian president backhandedly rebuffed Lula's optimism when he gave the initiative only a 30 percent chance of succeeding.[55] Nevertheless, subsequent negotiations on May 17 produced the so-called Tehran Declaration between Iran, Brazil, and Turkey under which Tehran agreed to transfer 1,200 kilograms of low enriched uranium to Turkey in return for 120 kilograms of 20 percent enriched uranium.[56] Still, Medvedev commented skeptically and pointedly about the amount of low enriched uranium that Iran was now offering to swap—proportionally considerably less than Iran had tentatively offered in October 2009, given Tehran's growing stockpile of low enriched uranium.[57] The very next day, May 18, a phone call between Secretary of State Hillary Clinton and Foreign Minister Lavrov finalized negotiations on a new sanctions measure among the P5+1 in the Security Council.[58]

In the Russian capital in mid-May 2010, a visitor found the general mood among Tehran-watchers to be disenchantment with Iran's recent behavior on the nuclear issue. Iran's attraction to Russia had been purely pragmatic, they said. Russia was a neighbor; and Iran had looked to Russia as a partner on the nuclear issue only because of the two countries' differences with the United States. These Iran analysts described Vladimir Putin as fed up with Ahmadinejad, and there was no expectation that relations would improve. A presidential apparat authority had claimed to one expert that the S–300 transfers would never go forward. The expert tended to agree. As he explained, the makers of the S–300 were interested in profits, but they had already gotten their money from the Russian government and their *baksheesh* (bribe) from Iranian contract negotiators.

Moreover, Russian observers claimed, the S–300 issue was of third rank importance to Putin and Medvedev. When they realized how important it was to the United States and Israel, they put delivery of the system on hold in an instant. Of course, it had helped that they were not happy with Iran. In the opinion of another expert, Putin and Medvedev took the interests of the arms and nuclear industries into account in framing policy toward Iran, but these sectors were not independent actors and broader interests prevailed. However, Moscow observers could not rule out that the S–300 transfers would eventually go forward. One argued that had Iran agreed to the TRR deal the previous fall, Russia would have gone ahead with the transfers. But now they were increasingly unlikely as long as Russia-U.S. relations continued to improve.[59]

As negotiations quickened that month on the final language of what would become known as UNSC Resolution 1929 (2010), Ahmadinejad quickly issued another shot across Moscow's bow that touched off an unprecedented exchange of high-level recriminations. On the margins of a cabinet meeting in Tehran, the Iranian president cautioned that "If I were in the place of Russian officials, I would be more careful in taking any actions and expressing opinions with regards to this great neighbor [Iran], and act more cautiously."[60] Several days later on May 26, during a visit to Kerman Province, he accused Russia, a historical friend, of siding with Iran's enemies. Addressing the Russian president directly, Ahmadinejad said, "Today, it is very difficult for us to justify the actions of Mr. Medvedev to the Iranian nation."[61]

Responding to Ahmadinejad's personal insult and anti-Russian invective, Medvedev continued to push the envelope of Russian commentary critical of Iran. On June 5, the Russian president issued one of the sharpest high-level Russian public reproaches of Iran in recent memory. Speaking at a news conference in Germany with Chancellor Angela Merkel, Medvedev confirmed that "sanctions have virtually been agreed" in UNSC negotiations on a new resolution. Expressing the hope that Iran would pay heed, Medvedev stated, "Irresponsible

The S–300 Contract: New Life, New Frustrations

Throughout 2000, with the Clinton administration limping toward its end, Russia moved toward abrogating the Gore-Chernomyrdin Commission ban on new Russian arms contracts with Iran that Chernomyrdin had signed in 1995. On November 3, 2000, Foreign Minister Igor Ivanov formally notified Washington that Russia would withdraw on December 1 from its pledge not to conclude any new contracts.[1]

In January 2001, the new Bush administration came to power in Washington. Though they now could have done so, the Russians nevertheless did not sign any significant new arms deals with Iran until the late November 2005 contract for the short range Tor-M1 (SA–15) air defense system.[2] The reasons probably included Putin's inclination to court the new Bush administration. This impulse was reinforced by developments after 9/11, when Putin agreed to U.S. and other Western bases in Central Asia to support the fight against the Taliban in Afghanistan. The Russian desire to work with the United States in the wake of 9/11 continued through 2002 and well into 2003.[3]

By September 2002, Iranian Defense Minister Ali Shamkhani complained bitterly in a newspaper interview that Russia did not want a stronger Iran and was selling Iran only weapons that would not provoke a reaction from America. "On the basis of their strategic assessment, [Russians] see the presence of a powerful country within the territorial geography a danger to Russian security. That is why they refrain even from selling defensive hardware and equipment to the Islamic Republic of Iran."[4]

[1] John W. Parker, *Persian Dreams: Moscow and Tehran Since the Fall of the Shah* (Washington, DC: Potomac Books, Inc., 2009), 142–144.
[2] In the meantime, the only reported deals were for 33 Mi-171 helicopters, three Su-25 attack planes, and three Mi-17V-5 in 2005. *Persian Dreams*, 146 and 212; and Konstantin Lantratov and Alexandra Gritskova, "Iran Shields Its Nuclear Activities by Russian Missiles," *Kommersant*, December 26, 2007, CEP20071226950405.
[3] *Persian Dreams*, 183–188, 213–216, 218–222.
[4] *Persian Dreams*, 213.

behavior cannot continue to be multiplied."[62] It was an expansion of the "irresponsible" theme that Medvedev had first used on April 27 in the Danish interview cited above.

Within days, the Security Council approved UNSC Resolution 1929 on June 9, 2010. The vote was 12 in favor, 2 (Turkey and Brazil) opposing, and 1 (Lebanon) abstaining. The resolution reinforced and expanded previous UNSC economic, technology, and military sanctions against Iran. It stepped up pressure on banking transactions, urged inspection of suspected cargo shipments, and recommended increased awareness regarding transactions by the Islamic Revolutionary Guard Corps and other entities and individuals involved in Iran's nuclear and ballistic missile programs. It retained language negotiated earlier banning eight categories of conventional arms but not explicitly the S–300 system.[63] It had earlier emerged that Russian negotiators had insisted that the draft text exempt the S–300 system from its weapons sales prohibitions.[64]

Coup de Grace: The S–300

Lavrov and his Foreign Ministry spokesman Andrey Nesterenko on June 10 implied and categorically stated, respectively, that the S–300 system was not covered by the resolution's restrictions.[65] The next day, however, Russia decided to turn the screws tighter on Tehran.[66] Moscow now appeared prepared to use the resolution as an excuse to prolong its freeze on S–300 transfers, even though it had negotiated a carve-out for the system in the list of weapons prohibited for transfer to Iran. In Paris on June 11, Putin reportedly underlined to Sarkozy Moscow's commitment not to transfer the S–300s.[67] In Moscow, an anonymous Kremlin source told journalists that the S–300 system fell under the new resolution's sanctions.[68]

In denying Iran the protection of the S–300 system, Moscow seemed intent on rebuffing Ahmadinejad's dismissal of UNSC Resolution 1929 as a "worthless paper."[69] Foreign policy expert Fedor Lukyanov argued that Moscow technically could still go ahead with the S–300 transfers sometime in the future should Tehran finally fully cooperate with the IAEA and thus lift the sanctions under which it now labored.[70] But for now, Lavrov on June 11 rubbed more salt on Tehran's wounds. At the annual SCO summit, this time held in Tashkent, Lavrov elaborated to the press on the summit's decision ruling out Iran becoming a full member of the SCO because it was under UNSC sanctions.[71] Surely knowing what was in store, Ahmadinejad skipped the meeting.

A month later, at a July 12 assembly of Russia's ambassadors in Moscow, Medvedev's treatment of Iran abandoned any diplomatic pretenses designed to give Russia and Iran wiggle room on the nuclear issue. "It is obvious that Iran is coming close to the possession of potential that could in principle be used to create nuclear weapons," the Russian president stated.[72] Ahmadinejad responded by calling Medvedev's remarks "an advertisement of a propaganda show, which is going to be performed by America." "Why does the Russian president want to have a role in this play?" asked the Iranian President. "We are sorry to see this. They should not be deceived."[73]

Lavrov devoted a special section on Iran in his annual tour d'horizon of Russian diplomacy at Moscow's State Institute of International Relations (MGIMO) in September 2010. Lavrov called on Iran to display the openness on its nuclear programs required by the IAEA: "We have repeatedly told our Iranian partners bluntly about this." While he criticized recent national sanctions against Iran not agreed to in the UNSC, he called on Iran to return to the October 2009 agreement on supplying fuel to the TRR. This step, he said, could constitute a confidence-building measure leading to further progress on the entire panoply of Iran's disputed nuclear enrichment program.[74]

There were subsequent hints that Tehran was preparing to respond by revisiting the TRR deal, as Lavrov had urged in his MGIMO remarks, using Iran's 20 percent enrichment capability as potential trade material in a negotiation.[75] In New York to attend the UN General Assembly on September 24, Ahmadinejad told a press conference that Iran would consider stopping enrichment to 20 percent when it felt "assured" over provision of fuel for the TRR. He again portrayed Iran's decision to enrich to 20 percent as having been forced on it by the "world powers" who had opposed Iran's counterproposal for a two-stage exchange of fuel.[76]

Earlier in Moscow, an unnamed high-level source told the Russian press that "It is unrealistic to demand that Iran reject enrichment of uranium to a level of 4 percent." The source, reportedly in the Russian leadership, argued that "We must concentrate on coming to agreement on rejecting enrichment to a level of up to 20 percent—this is the level that makes it possible to develop a bomb." Lavrov at the same time told the press that it would probably be a good idea for the P5+1 to take another look at their basic approach to Iran to make sure that it "adequately reflect[s] the realities that exist today."[77]

However, in the absence of any concrete moves by Tehran, Russian suspicion of Iran's nuclear program and regional ambitions remained high, as did Russian incentives to work more closely with the United States against the common threat. The tough decree that Medvedev issued on September 22, spelling out Russian sanctions of Iran pursuant to UNSC Resolution 1929, including nontransfer of the S–300 system, was intended to reinforce the point.[78] Despite hopes in Tehran that relations with Moscow would improve, and concerns by some observers in Moscow that relations with Washington were bound to deteriorate, Medvedev's September 22 edict on implementing Resolution 1929 stunningly suggested a determination in the Kremlin that it be otherwise.

Medvedev's directive, together with its four annexes, banned the export to Iran, including through third countries or from third countries through Russia, of any tanks, armored vehicles, large-caliber artillery systems, warplanes, combat helicopters, warships, missiles, or missile systems as defined by the UN Conventional Arms Register, as well as the S–300 air defense system, and of any material means associated with all these weapons, including spare parts. The edict also banned 14 specific individuals connected with Iran's nuclear and or possibly related missile programs from entering or transiting Russia, prohibited the provision of any financial services to any operations connected to these same Iranian programs, and proscribed any operations connected with them by assets or resources on Russian territory.[79]

Medvedev's decree caused the freezing or cancellation of most Russian weapons contracts with Iran. However, five agreements reportedly fell outside the sanctions regime and continued, according to an unnamed military-diplomatic source in Moscow. But of the five, the source would specify only that for Krasnopol high-precision laser-guided artillery shells.[80] A year later, seemingly scraping the bottom of the barrel, the sale of a batch of radio electronic combat systems was also reported.[81]

As to whether the S–300 contract would actually be torn up or simply suspended, General Nikolay Makarov, head of the General Staff, who made the initial announcement of Medvedev's edict, told reporters on September 22 that "We shall see; this will depend on Iran's behavior."[82] Just 2 weeks later, however, Sergey Chemezov, head of the Russian Technologies State Corporation, announced the cancellation of the S–300 contract.[83] Chemezov put Russia's monetary liability for breaking the contract at no more than $166.8 million, the amount he claimed that Russia had received in advance.[84] The amount was eventually repaid, but that did not stop Iran from suing Russia in the International Court of Justice over the broken contract, to Moscow's clear irritation.[85]

In Moscow, Iranian Ambassador Seyyed Mahmoud-Reza Sajjadi cautioned that Russia's decision to cancel its contractual obligations to sell arms to Iran would lose it not only the Iranian market but its markets in other countries as well. He noted that the people-to-people relationship between Russia and Iran was better than the government-to-government relationship but that the S–300 decision was having a "very negative effect" on public opinion toward Russia in Iran.[86] In Tehran, Defense Minister Ahmad Vahidi said that Iran would pursue compensation for the broken S–300 contract and warned that Moscow's decision would hurt Russian interests.[87]

In the provincial capital of Bojnord, Ahmadinejad insinuated that Satan had influenced Russia to cancel the S–300, insisted the contract was still valid and Russia should honor it, and warned that if Russia did not, then Iran would pursue damages and compensation.[88] All in all, relations appeared to have deteriorated to levels not seen since the mid-1980s after the Soviet Union invaded Afghanistan and supported Iraq in war against Iran, and after the new Iranian Islamic revolutionary government decimated the Soviet-supported Tudeh communist party.

Debate Over Sanctions

As Russian-Iranian relations deteriorated in spring 2010, sanctions were the subject of debates in Moscow. Hardliners called for toughening Russia's stance while others saw Iran as a good card to play against the United States.

Most observers in Moscow supported what one analyst described as Russia's "cold-blooded" determination to have "good and friendly" relations with Iran. This thinker listed areas for cooperation over the next 10 years as trade, gas transit, and coordination on regional issues. Among the latter, he pointed to common interests in fighting the narcotics traffic out of Afghanistan, and the need for Russia, China, India, and Iran to work together in Afghanistan as the United States leaves. The U.S. withdrawal from Iraq would require similar Russian coordination with Iran and other regional powers.[89]

After passage of UNSC Resolution 1929, the mainstream analytical—but not official—view in Moscow was that it had been unwise for Russia to sign up to the resolution's tough sanctions. The consensus view was that excessive toughening of sanctions undermined Russia's economic interests and damaged its image in Iran. Most argued that it was necessary not only to pressure Tehran but also to give it room to retreat and compromise and not back it into a corner.[90]

Contrary to the frequent perception among outside observers of robust economic ties,[91] Russian-Iranian bilateral trade has been modest for years—even before Resolution 1929. One close analyst noted that the $3.1 billion recorded in 2009 was outpaced by Iran's trade with China ($27 billion) and even Germany and Italy ($5–8 billion).[92] As relations plummeted in 2010, the pro-Iran commentator Rajab Safarov called for a "strategic union" between Moscow and Tehran.[93] The more critical Vladimir Sazhin, however, argued that there was not a "strong enough basis" for this. He pointed out that Russia's trade with Iran was little more than Russia's trade with Israel, whose population was a tenth the size of Iran.[94]

In May 2010, other observers noted that Russian companies such as Lukoil and Gazprom were leaving or suspending operations in Iran over fears of sanctions and unpredictability on the Iranian side. They claimed that a lot of the talk about Russian-Iranian cooperation on energy issues was simply "bluff." Experts admitted that most Russian banks did not want to deal with Iran because of unpredictability.[95] In one well-publicized case, Iran finally expelled Gazprom Neft from a project to develop the Azar oilfield after the Russian company repeatedly slowed the project.[96]

Experts opposed to harsher sanctions asserted that Iran was ready to develop mutually profitable cooperation with Russia in all spheres, but was holding back because of Russia's inability or unwillingness to fulfill bilateral agreements, including the S–300 contract. Several other experts, however, discounted the existence any longer of a strong and open pro-Iran lobby in Russia. It now existed only on the fringes, they asserted, unlike in the 1990s, when corrupt politicians such as the Liberal Democratic Party's Vladimir Zhirinovskiy and the Communists received bribes from the Iranians.[97] Tellingly, Russia was backing out of the S–300 contract even as it reeled from the global financial crisis and its gross domestic product dropped 7.8 percent in 2009, the sharpest contraction among the G–20 countries.

A year later, bilateral trade was still depressed. In September 2011, a report surfaced of talks on a $1–1.2 billion megadeal for a joint venture between Iran's Bank Saderat and Russia's Rostekhnologii to develop the world's largest lead and zinc deposit in Iran.[98] A separate news story asserted that negotiations were under way between Russia's Rusal aluminum conglomerate and Iran's Mines and Mining Industries Development and Renovation Organization about the possibility of building an aluminum plant in Iran that would produce the equivalent of 9 percent of Rusal's current capacity.[99] Neither project, however, appeared remotely close to contractual closing, due to the usual protracted haggling by the Iranian side and Russian misgivings over running afoul of UNSC sanctions.

In November 2011, as Russia protested the most recent report by the IAEA on Iran's nuclear enrichment program, Putin demonstratively asked Rosatom chief Sergey Kiriyenko whether Iran had "not expressed the wish to continue the construction of new units [at Bushehr]?" "Yes, it has," responded Kiriyenko, adding that Rosatom already had the "relevant instruction" and was formulating proposals.[100] A week later, however, Kiriyenko admitted that no negotiations were going on.[101] Similarly, in December, Iranian television announced a $1 billion contract between Iran's Petroleum Engineering and Development Company and Russia's Tatneft Company to develop the Zagheh heavy oilfield in southwestern Iran near the port of Deylam.[102] Hours later, Tehran was embarrassed when Tafneft denied it had signed such a deal.[103]

As Lukoil vice president Leonid Fedun put it to journalists when describing his own company's approach to Iran, "Operations in Iran are still interesting for us but, as you know, there are sanctions in effect there."[104] A Russian analyst explained in July 2011 that Russian business elites are not rushing to Iran because they are more oriented toward Europe and do not want hassles from sanctions. Only 0.2 percent of Russian firms are involved in Iran.

This was a big problem in trying to raise trade levels, which this analyst put significantly lower than reported earlier: $1.8 billion in 2008 and $1.9 billion in 2009. In 2010, it was $2.8 billion, and in 2011 it would be slightly greater. (Another observer called this "miserable," just enough for Russia to demonstrate to Iran that the two countries were not enemies.) The bulk of trade is in metal, steel, wood products, and machine tools. In the energy sector, Russian and Iranian interests are too competitive to allow for cooperation. In contrast, there are 5,000 German firms active in Iran, and the Chinese are involved in a big way in the Iranian market.[105] According to China's ambassador to Iran, bilateral trade was $30 billion in 2010 and would probably reach $40 billion in 2011.[106]

An elder statesman noted in February 2011 that Russia had no strong economic interests in a solution to the Iranian nuclear problem because the two countries were energy-producing competitors. Once sanctions were removed, Iran would compete for the European energy market and buy commercial airliners from the United States rather than Russia. Yet it remained in Russia's interests to maintain good relations with Iran and avoid a political crisis, which could lead to an immediate negative reaction from Iran in the Caucasus especially.

At the same time, as the two capitals tried to recover and stabilize the relationship in early 2011, another expert critical of Iran argued that the United States and the Europeans should continue sanctions even though Moscow might oppose them. His rationale was that sanctions would maintain the technological gap between Iran's present capabilities and the capacity necessary to produce a nuclear weapon. Moreover, Iran's many domestic and regional vulnerabilities opened up windows of opportunity through which to pressure the regime, which could not go on forever, and to slow down its nuclear and missile programs.[107]

In April 2011, the Oriental Institute held a conference on Iran sanctions. According to one account, Nina Mamedova, head of the institute's Iran department, concluded in her presentation that "A further toughening of sanctions could influence the position of Iran's leadership toward its nuclear program, especially if the application of sanctions is not in any way linked to efforts to change the regime itself."[108] A young scholar, Nikolay Kozhanov, published a detailed analysis that found sanctions were having some impact on Iran's energy sector, but cautioned that the United States and the European Union (EU) would have to be patient and persistent for sanctions to have the desired effect on Iranian policy. At the same time, Kozhanov pointed out that Iran still had considerable room for maneuver, particularly by expanding trade with China, Malaysia, Turkey, Turkmenistan, Brazil, Venezuela, Pakistan, and various African countries.[109]

In July 2011, some long-time Iran experts observed that sanctions *were* working, though they had not yet had a significant impact on Iran's nuclear program. Iran would continue to find loopholes in the sanctions regime, but this was becoming more difficult. Sanctions created public unhappiness, but they also unified the regime. According to these experts' contacts in Tehran, however, those in power were tired of the nuclear enrichment issue and wanted to solve it. The economic costs of the program were high and they would like to lower them. But Iranian politics did not allow a solution that included renouncing nuclear enrichment.[110]

Ties Bad but Manageable

All the same, since ties reached their low point in 2010, Moscow and Tehran have been trying to lift them. Both sides are making sure that they continue to have active channels of

The S–300 Contract: Negotiations Go Forward

International pressure mounted on Iran in August 2002 with assertions of vast nuclear program construction sites at Arak and Natanz.[1] After subsequent revelations, Iran finally on October 21, 2003, delivered to the IAEA what it claimed was a "full disclosure" of its past and present nuclear enrichment activities.[2]

Then, on November 10, Iran's top nuclear negotiator Hasan Rowhani announced in Moscow that Iran was ready voluntarily to suspend nuclear enrichment activities and to sign an IAEA safeguards Additional Protocol.[3]

Putin responded during his meeting with Rowhani that since Iran was exercising "self-restraint," "I do not see any obstacle to our cooperation with Iran in the nuclear sphere."[4]

The next day, the first of several press stories appeared asserting that it had been Tehran's secret nuclear program that had up until then blocked Moscow from entering into new arms contracts with Iran. Since Tehran was about to sign an Additional Protocol with the IAEA, Putin reportedly was now willing to move forward on new contract negotiations.[5]

---

[1] John W. Parker, *Persian Dreams: Moscow and Tehran Since the Fall of the Shah* (Washington, DC: Potomac Books, Inc., 2009), 216–217.

[2] *Persian Dreams*, 253.

[3] *Persian Dreams*, 253.

[4] Moscow Channel One TV, November 10, 2003, CEP20031110000113.

[5] Ivan Safronov, "Tehran Requests Fire Power. Russia Prepared to Begin Massive Deliveries of Weapons to Iran," *Kommersant*, November 12, 2003, CEP20031112000180; and Sami Imarah, "Putin Informed Rowhani of Russia's Willingness to Resume Supplying Iran with Arms," *Asharq al-Awsat* (London), November 13, 2003, GMP20031114000144.

---

communication, even though the substance of their engagement through these channels often appears to be pretty thin gruel.

On the eve of passage in the UNSC of Resolution 1929, Putin committed Russia to commissioning the Bushehr nuclear power plant that August, a move clearly designed to assuage public opinion in Iran toward Russia.[111] Even as Tehran waited for Medvedev to issue his implementation decree and decide the fate of the S–300 contract after adoption of UNSC Resolution 1929, both sides tried to use the ceremony marking the launch of preparations to load fuel at Bushehr, even if some 10 years behind schedule, to cool off the rhetoric. Ironically, given the bad press in Iran that the delay had gained Russia over the years, the fuel-loading and preparations for generating electricity from Bushehr began to carry much of the weight for this attempt to improve relations. The nuclear power plant continued to serve that function even as repeated snafus postponed its power-generation startup until September 2011.[112]

Within weeks of cancellation of the S–300 contract, Ahmadinejad's chief of staff, Esfandiar Rahim Mashaei, asserted that "Iran-Russia relations are not strained and it is the countries' interests which determine political ties."[113] In Moscow, Iranian Ambassador Sajjadi claimed that regardless of what had happened recently, both countries were trying to improve their mutual relations.[114] A week later, he urged that "We must not think that the Iranian-Russian relations are in a critical stage but should pay due attention to the future of our relations."[115] A month later, the ambassador said that Iranians were not happy that Russia was not fulfilling its obligations, but relations with Russia were "more important" than the S–300 contract.[116] The same day, Ahmadinejad seemed to signal a desire for a truce when he stated that "we call for bilateral cooperation and assistance."[117]

Overall, Tehran appeared to be the *demandeur* and Moscow the coolly reluctant target of Iranian pursuit. Iran tried to play on Russian expert and public opinion that was uneasy over Moscow's approval of UNSC Resolution 1929 and Medvedev's cancellation of the S–300 contract. In October 2010, responding to a Russian interviewer's assertion that "the overwhelming majority of Russians did not support Medvedev's decision to impose sanctions against Iran and also that the Russian people are for closer cooperation with Iran," Sajjadi said that he was "very happy that the Russian people have the same assessment of this matter as I do."[118]

Three months later, in January 2011, the ambassador hewed to his public diplomacy campaign when he hosted a reception for 50 well-known Russian bloggers.[119] When an Iranian parliamentary delegation visited Moscow at the end of the month, the group made a pitch for Iranian assistance to Russia's "serious involvement" in the Middle East in exchange for Russia's helping Iran establish a "serious presence" in the Caucasus and in the SCO, where it only had observer status. Yet the Iranian delegation went home empty-handed, complaining that Russian politicians were not committed to improving the relationship.[120]

In early 2011, the view in Moscow was that everyone knew that Iran did not like or trust Russians. Cancellation of the S–300 contract had been the end of the line. Among the Iranian people there was not even elementary respect for Russia. According to some long-time observers of Iran in the Russian capital, this fact troubled some leaders in Tehran, who wanted to improve Russia's standing among Iranians and, therefore, opposed the line that Russia did not deserve trust. Among them were pragmatists who believed Iran and Russia still shared some common interests. But there were also those who tried to befriend Russia only in order to benefit Iran.

One well-placed Russian observer succinctly summarized the view that this writer encountered in multiple interviews with officials and analysts in Moscow in February 2011: relations between Moscow and Tehran were "bad." Iran was extremely irritated by the Russian position. Tehran knew it had become the subject of tradeoffs between Moscow and Washington. At the same time, it was difficult to think that Russia would go any further on sanctions without a serious new tradeoff offer from Washington to Moscow.

In any event, in this Moscow observer's view, a new chapter was beginning. In Tehran, there was possibly the hope and perhaps even already the expectation that Putin would move back to the presidency in 2012. In Moscow, the view was that Russia's position vis-à-vis Iran was a function of the U.S.-Russia relationship. What if there were no quick success in missile defense talks or if Russia's World Trade Organization bid stalled? An extreme scenario for Russia's reaction would be the resurrection of the S–300 deal with Iran, this observer mused, although he immediately added that would be too ridiculous and was therefore unlikely. Therefore, he concluded, Russia and Iran would march in place for the next 6 months to a year, but at the same time Russia would not agree with the United States and other Western P5+1 members to a new round of sanctions.

Similarly, another analyst portrayed both sides as exhausted with each other. Russia had practically nothing to show from its ties to Iran. Russia had claimed that it had an independent position and relationship with Iran, but this assertion now meant nothing in the wake of cancellation of the S–300 contract. Yet another long-time observer of Russia's relations with Iran seemed to draw satisfaction by what he detected as the official Moscow consensus on Iran beginning to waver on the issue of sanctions. Russia now understood, he asserted, that "enough is enough."[121]

In fact, Moscow began increasingly to criticize unilateral U.S. and EU sanctions against Iran that went beyond those agreed in UNSC Resolution 1929. By February 2011, this Russian criticism developed into outright opposition to another round of UNSC sanctions. On February 15, Foreign Minister Lavrov declared in London that UNSC Resolution 1929 had "exhausted virtually all the opportunities to apply sanctions to those involved, even indirectly, in the Iranian nuclear program. Any further sanctions would mean the strangling of Iran's economy and the creation of social problems for its population." Russia, therefore, would be "unable to support" additional sanctions against Iran.[122]

Unstated was that Moscow's refusal to contemplate more sanctions was in effect an attempt to regain at least the semblance of distance from the U.S. position and thus somewhat repair Russia's relationship with Iran. Moscow and Tehran began ostentatiously to reengage in at least pro forma talks on a variety of issues, an effort that continues to this day.

The Engagement Imperative

In February 2011, a former senior diplomat counseled against isolating Iran. There was a need to speak now to Ahmadinejad and others in power, not wait for the opposition to replace them. There was no unanimity in the Iranian leadership, so there was a need for permanent contacts in order to ascertain intra-regime differences and play on them. It was in Russia's interests to maintain good relations with Iran. Iran's active policy was directed toward the Gulf, Middle East, and Afghanistan, not north toward Russia.

All the same, this elder statesman did not want to exaggerate outside leverage on Iran. The Iranians, he noted, thought they were more clever than others and could influence them, not the reverse. Nevertheless, it was necessary to start a broader dialogue with Iran on regional issues. If this were not done, the Iranians would try to use other forces—Hizballah and the Muslim Brotherhood, among others—to interfere throughout the Middle East.[123]

Even when Russo-Iranian tensions were at their highest, Ahmadinejad and Medvedev met on the margins of the Caspian summit in Baku in November 2010, on the eve of Medvedev's participation in the Lisbon NATO summit at which he pledged that Russia would explore cooperation with NATO on missile defense in Europe.[124] According to one report, the Iranian president emerged frowning from the meeting, which Medvedev aide Sergey Prikhodko described as "candid" and not avoiding "awkward questions."[125] Medvedev later said that he had used the meeting to impress on his counterpart that Iran must prove that its nuclear program was peaceful and that it was ready to cooperate with the IAEA.[126] Following that, the two presidents spoke by phone in January and March and met at the SCO summit in Astana in June 2011.[127]

At lower levels, Tehran especially has gone out of its way to advertise bilateral consultations with Moscow on energy,[128] transportation,[129] communications,[130] trade,[131] financial crime,[132] narcotrafficking,[133] terrorism,[134] Afghanistan,[135] and even Syria.[136] Even on Caspian issues, where the key point of seabed delimitation remains unresolved, the subject is one on which both sides can at least underscore continuing contacts, including a next summit scheduled for Moscow.[137]

Russian observers in early 2011 judged that Ahmadinejad's position had somewhat strengthened. From their vantage point in Moscow, they had never set much store in the ability of the Green Movement to change the domestic leadership landscape in Iran. The election struggle was already beginning for the next president and the next Majles, they pointed out. In the process, Ahmadinejad was reinventing himself as a great Iranian nationalist, and the prospects for Green Movement success were fairly low.[138]

Indeed, as Green Movement pressure on Ahmadinejad eased in 2010, the Iranian president took the bit in his teeth against those opponents who had attached themselves to the street protestors: presidential challenger Mousavi, former parliamentary chairman Mehdi Karoubi, former president Mohammad Khatami, and former president and current chairman of the Assembly of Experts Ali Akbar Hashemi Rafsanjani. By February 2011, Ahmadinejad had succeeded in forcing all of them into house arrest and/or political limbo.[139]

However, the president did not have long to savor his victories as he pushed forward to prepare for parliamentary elections in June 2012. These would be an important preliminary to presidential elections in 2013, in which the president was constitutionally prohibited from running for a third term but had great incentives for arranging to put the succession into the hands of a supporter.

Instead, with Supreme Leader Khamenei's support, Ahmadinejad's many opponents within the establishment redoubled their attacks on him.[140] The turmoil in Iranian domestic politics did not obstruct efforts by officials in both Moscow and Tehran to be seen as engaged with each other and pursuing common neighborly interests. However, with Khamenei repeatedly clipping Ahmadinejad's wings, there seemed to be little chance in the near-term of the president's revisiting the TRR deal or launching some other high-profile nuclear initiative with either Moscow or Washington.

Whether in the bilateral context with Russia, or in the Vienna Group venue that worked out the stillborn October 2009 TRR deal, or in the full P5+1 format, Iran had earlier hinted several times that the issue of 20 percent enrichment was negotiable although not the issue of enrichment to 3–4 percent. Since the disputed elections of June 2009, however, the nuclear issue had proved a third rail in Iranian politics. Most detractors of Ahmadinejad seemed resolved to deny him any room to compromise, whether with the United States or with Russia. From Green Movement leaders Mousavi and Karoubi to Majles Speaker Ali Larijani, they all hoisted Ahmadinejad on his own nuclear petard when he showed any willingness to strike a deal potentially curbing Iran's nuclear enrichment program in any way.

Facing such political gridlock in Tehran, Moscow's only rational course of action seemed to be to march in place while continuing to engage Tehran on a variety of issues, even if with little in the way of concrete results to show for its efforts. Moreover, poor personal relations at the top had affected Russian-Iranian ties, and they had become much more complicated. The only exception to this bleak picture was the Bushehr nuclear power station, where Russian contractors were finally nearing completion of the project.

In February 2011, as Lavrov began to oppose a new round of sanctions and in July 2011 trotted out Russia's "step-by-step" initiative, no one in Moscow saw either member of the current ruling tandem as a fan of Iran.[141] The publicity Moscow gave step-by-step was restrained. Russia's rulers appeared inclined to see Ahmadinejad's Iran as more of a threat than it had been under predecessor Khatami. In Washington, State Department spokesperson Victoria Nuland said Washington had worked with Moscow on the step-by-step proposal and that "We welcome any Russian effort to persuade Iran that it's time to change course and meet its international obligations."[142]

In Tehran, however, Ahmadinejad and his supporters once again seemed to appreciate the potential value of Russian diplomacy in blocking additional international sanctions even as Ahmadinejad appeared increasingly to be in political eclipse. Tehran responded with a vaguely worded counterproposal offering IAEA inspectors "full supervision" of Iran's nuclear activities for 5 years.[143] But the vagueness of the response suggested that Tehran simply wanted to remain engaged in endless talks while continuing to move ahead on its nuclear enrichment program. It may also have masked the unrelenting brutal political infighting in Tehran.[144] In addition, views appeared split in Tehran on the prospects of working any further with Russia. Majles Foreign Relations Committee chairman Heshmatollah Felahatpisheh charged that Russia had distanced itself from Iran and was responsible for the nuclear file's referral to the UN Security Council.[145]

However, in the event that Tehran decided to take a more cooperative tack on the nuclear issue, it could well again signal its preparedness for compromise through Moscow. That had happened in November 2003 when Iran Security Council head Hassan Rowhani, in a Kremlin meeting with Putin, had formally announced Iran's temporary and voluntary suspension of nuclear enrichment activities and its agreement to sign an additional protocol to the Non-Proliferation Treaty (NPT).[146]

Should something comparable now happen once again, Moscow could declare it a victory for Russia's policy of engagement, much as it did in 2003 when Rowhani met with Putin. Having gone against the grain of expert and public opinion in 2010 on its sanctions and S–300 decisions, any Kremlin backtracking from them would meet little resistance. To the contrary, it would probably be welcomed since it would be going with the flow of mainstream expert and public opinion rather than against it. That certainly seemed to be the case when Moscow, in February 2011, began publicly to state its opposition to any more international sanctions against Iran.[147]

Taking Stock and Peering Ahead

Assuming no change in Tehran, however, several experts speculated in July 2011 that if Putin returned to the presidency he could adjust policy to be more balanced, but they did not think it would change significantly. All experts said that Moscow regarded the S–300 decision as a tool to influence Washington and part of an implicit package that included missile defense.

If "reset" did not advance, then Russia would go back to using relations with Iran as leverage on U.S. policy. Many were downbeat on the outcome of ongoing upheavals in the Middle East. Several experts saw Iran as an important beneficiary of the Arab Spring. Others were more tentative, seeing the region as still in flux.[148]

In the meantime, among the expert community in Moscow, several analysts had focused well before this on how to deter a nuclear Iran and prevent it from becoming a regional bully once it became a nuclear power. One had suggested that the ultimate future counter to a nuclear Iran might have to be NATO Article 5–type guarantees by the United States, Russia, and perhaps also China to Iran's threatened neighbors, including Israel and Saudi Arabia. This analyst saw a strategic security alliance with the United States as the best outcome for Russia from the current "reset" process.[149]

Surveying Tehran politics in July 2011, most experts in Moscow saw no good outcomes, only a choice between the bad and the terrible. They were downbeat on what to do. While supporting a carrot-and-stick policy, they called it useless at the moment because they foresaw no movement in Tehran on the nuclear issue until at least after the Iranian parliamentary elections in June 2012.[150] For the time being, Moscow seemed to be handling Iran with a showy readiness for engagement masking a series of polite brush-offs.

Looking at Tehran, Moscow in summer 2011 could not be sure what it would face in 2012 or after except that it would not be good. Ahmadinejad seemed on the ropes, and there was no clear successor. Ahmadinejad's election in 2005 had been a surprise, and his fraud-filled reelection in 2009 had weakened his hand. His presidency had ultimately been a disappointment for Moscow's hopes of guiding Tehran to a compromise on its nuclear enrichment program and improving relations.

At the SCO summit in Astana in June 2011, which Ahmadinejad attended after skipping the previous year's session, Medvedev seemed to put some distance between himself and his Iranian counterpart. Medvedev did not meet with him one-on-one. Instead, the Russian president saw Ahmadinejad in an expanded threesome with Kazakhstani leader Nursultan Nazarbayev. According to Lavrov, Medvedev at this meeting called for more constructive Iranian interaction with the P5+1 and greater transparency with the IAEA.[151] At least some in Tehran seemed to get the message. Two months later, Foreign Minister Ali Akbar Salehi would describe the Astana meeting as "a new landmark and page in relations."[152]

All this suggested that Moscow, while not moving on to additional sanctions, would not move rashly to roll back its UNSC Resolution 1929 sanctions until Iranian politics clarified themselves and Tehran took steps toward compromise on the nuclear issue. Under those conditions, the step-by-step initiative seemed a good tactic. It allowed Moscow to remain engaged and repair relations with Iran while at the same time gently pressuring and probing Tehran's intentions as well as burnishing Russia's own credentials as a mediator—though careful not to presume that Tehran would respond with concrete steps.

Evolving Assessment of the Iranian Nuclear Threat

In recent years, as Tehran has resisted efforts by the IAEA to get to the bottom of unanswered questions about its nuclear enrichment program and evidence has surfaced that Iran has explored aspects of nuclear weaponization, expert opinion in Moscow has become more cognizant of the potential Iranian threat to Russian interests. A distinct minority still adheres to the view that there is no hard evidence that Iran is going nuclear and that Iran should be presumed innocent until proven guilty. However, few now doubt that Iran has a military nuclear program and a ballistic missile program to go along with it.

The Russian Foreign Ministry criticized the November 8, 2011, IAEA report on Iran for "juggling with information in order to create an impression that the Iranian nuclear program allegedly has a military component."[153] All the same, the Russian leadership and most experts in Moscow have no illusions on this score. In July 2010, as we have seen, Medvedev clearly stated that "It is obvious that Iran is coming close to the possession of potential that could in principle be used to create nuclear weapons."[154] More recently, on November 18, 2011, Defense Minister Anatoly Serdyukov told the press that Russia wants to continue leasing the Qabala early warning radar in Azerbaijan and intends to upgrade it. Enhancing the capacity of Qabala, Serdyukov said, is "useful and very important, in particular given the Iranian [missile] program."[155] The same day, materials prepared for a report by General Makarov, head of the General Staff, reportedly included the buildup of Iran's nuclear potential among developments that could draw Russia's armed forces into a future conflict.[156]

Most experts interviewed by this author over the past 2 years believe that Iran will eventually attain the potential to build a "bomb in the cellar," although they see Tehran as unlikely to take the political decision actually to produce a nuclear weapon until it judges it politically necessary. However, not many are confident that Iran will not cross the "stop and hide" threshold, and some are concerned that Iran will proceed directly and openly to producing an actual nuclear device à la North Korea, thus scuttling the NPT.[157]

Overall, experts in Moscow do not judge Iran to be as close to producing a nuclear weapon as is believed in the West. The timelines one hears range from 5 to 10 years.[158] Even after the most recent IAEA report, an unimpressed Vladimir Sazhin of the Oriental speculated that it would still take 5 to 7 years for Iran to marry a workable warhead with a capable missile—if there were no outside interference.[159]

One expert cautions that Iran will probably stop dealing with the IAEA only when it has overcome all technical problems and has all the inputs necessary to produce a bomb and a delivery vehicle. Only at that point, when Iran stops negotiating with the IAEA, argues this expert, can one talk about when Iran will produce its first nuclear weapon. Realistically, Iran would need to produce at least three to five warheads, and not just one, to allow for testing and breakdowns. This expert estimates that Iran would need at least 2 years after a decision to break with the IAEA to produce three warheads.[160]

In the meantime, the view of most Russian experts is that IAEA control of Iran's nuclear program is more important than how much uranium Iran has enriched. In this connection, one expert urged resolution of the TRR fuel problem even if only in exchange for one-third of Iran's current low enriched uranium stock as long as Iran's nuclear program is kept strictly under IAEA control. All observers think that Iran's withdrawal from the NPT would be dangerous and the world community should do everything to keep it in.[161]

When it comes to missile delivery systems, the view of one expert is that Iran is not well prepared yet but is on its way. The Iranians are always trying to confuse and fool outsiders, but in reality they do not yet have a solid-fuel launch-ready rocket to deliver a nuclear warhead. The Shahab-3, first tested in 1998, is a one-stage liquid-fuel missile that requires hours of preparation to fire, so is quite vulnerable. However, the newer two-stage solid-fuel Sejil, which will replace the Shahab-3, will be a good delivery vehicle when it is deployed.[162] With a 1,000-kilogram warhead, the Sejil has a range of 2,200 kilometers; with a 500-kilogram warhead, it has a range of 3,000 kilometers.

In the opinion of military and foreign policy expert Vladimir Yevseyev, Sejil will present a potential threat to a number of European countries and southern districts of Russia when it becomes operational in 2 years.[163] According to retired Major-General Vladimir Dvorkin, the time Iran will need to deploy enhanced-range ballistic missiles will be roughly the same as that projected for the United States and NATO to deploy a missile defense system in Europe.

However, Deputy Defense Minister Anatoliy Antonov, Moscow's lead negotiator on New START (Strategic Arms Reduction Treaty) and now on missile defense, has stated that "We are carefully monitoring the development of [Iran's] missile potential, but our estimates of Iran's missile capabilities still differ from the estimates that exist in NATO. We think that today, the only thing we can talk about is something potential rather than real."[164]

Moreover, in the estimation of many analysts, there do not exist sufficient antagonisms to provoke Tehran to use Sejil against Europe, although Tehran no doubt views Sejil as necessary against Israel.[165] Nevertheless, technically competent Iran-watchers in Moscow—such as

Yevseyev and Dvorkin—are beginning to argue that, with growing Iranian capability to target Europe in the future, Russia should not give Iran a pass on intent.[166]

Some experts do recognize the indirect threats to Russian security interests resulting from a nuclear and missile arms race in the Middle East provoked by Iranian achievements or from instability in Iran and the Middle East resulting from a U.S. and/or Israeli strike on Iranian nuclear facilities.[167] In addition, there has long been concern in Moscow over the potential for mischief by Iran along Russia's southern periphery and especially in Russia's North Caucasus.[168]

Still, for a variety of reasons, it is hard to find anyone in the Russian capital who fears an Iranian missile strike. At the same time, the Russian public does not view Iran as exceptionally hostile to Russia. In fact, by some polling results, Russians view the United States as more antagonistic than Iran to Russian interests. In May 2011, only 7 percent of respondents included Iran among the 5 countries most unfriendly to Russia compared to 33 percent who included the United States.[169] A year earlier, 55 percent saw the stationing of American missile defense systems in countries bordering on Russia as the bigger threat compared to only 13 percent who perceived the Iranian nuclear program in similar terms.[170]

Among Iran-watchers in Moscow, nobody wants a nuclear Iran, but Russians do not see an Iran with nuclear weapons as posing an existential problem for Russia. It would be a bad development, they agree, but Russia could live with it. The view is widespread that it is in Russia's interests to keep patiently engaged with Iran however far Iran goes down the path of nuclear militarization.[171] Should Iran attain nuclear status, the prediction is that the international community will continue to deal with it much as it did with Pakistan after it obtained nuclear weapons: nothing much will happen, and relations will continue.[172]

Central Asia and Caucasus: Eternal Worries

Part of Russia's approach toward Iran is defensive and driven by concern that Iran might support Islamic militants in Central Asia and especially closer to home in Russia's North Caucasus territories with their significant Muslim populations. It is especially important to Russians that Iran not support anti-Russian elements in the Caucasus and Central Asia.[173] Glossing over Iran's role in the Tajik civil war in 1992, however, most analysts in Moscow claim that Iran has never hurt Russian interests in Central Asia and the North Caucasus.[174]

Most observers in Moscow agree that Russian-Iranian ties are important for the future stability of these regions.[175] Several experts, however, dispute the view that Shia Iran could pose a threat to these areas, where the Muslim communities are overwhelmingly Sunni. All the same, a number of these communities have cultural, linguistic, and historical links to the Persian

The S–300 Contract: Deal Clinched

After Rowhani's November 2003 visit to Moscow, any new arms deals soon got bogged down in Russia's reaction to a new round of revelations about Iran's nuclear activities, this time over Iran's dealings with Pakistani nuclear scientist Abdul Qadeer Khan going back to 1987.[1]

Nevertheless, talks finally began to produce results in late spring 2004—it would later be revealed—on a new contract that would include both the Tor-M1 and the S–300 air defense systems.

From Moscow's point of view, Iranian behavior had begun to improve. Iran had answered some—but not all—of the IAEA's questions and then on November 15, 2004, signed an agreement in Paris voluntarily "to continue and extend" suspension of nuclear enrichment activities.[2]

At the same time, Moscow's relations with Washington had come off their high point of 2002, battered by the U.S.-led invasion of Iraq in March 2003, and "color revolutions" in Georgia, Ukraine, and Kyrgyzstan.[3]

By July 2005, Putin endorsed—orchestrated?—the SCO summit call for Operation *Enduring Freedom* members to "set final deadlines for the temporary use" of bases in Central Asia to support operations in Afghanistan. That set the stage for Tashkent to demand that the United States abandon the Karshi-Khanabad air base in southern Uzbekistan.[4]

Then, on December 5, 2005, Sergei Ivanov confirmed news reports that Moscow had just signed a contract to deliver about 30 Tor-M1 air defense systems in the next 2 years.[5]

One Russian publication's "confidential sources" asserted that Moscow would begin deliveries as early as January 2006, despite U.S. objections, upon Iranian "pre-payment of several hundred million dollars."[6] However, without the long-range S–300 to work alongside the short-range Tor-M1s, which have limited defensive capability, fulfillment of the contract seemed to be a political gesture.[7]

Consequently, on December 26, 2007, while visiting Moscow, Iranian Defense Minister Mohammad Najjar spilled the beans when he told the press that "S–300 air defense systems will be supplied to Iran within the framework of an agreement earlier concluded with Russia."[8] There were several detailed accounts in the Russian media of negotiations over the system going back to 2004.[9] Anonymous Russian defense industry sources said that the contract negotiations were now in their final stages and that S–300 transfers would begin in 2008.[10]

The S–300 Contract: Deal Clinched (cont.)

[1] John W. Parker, *Persian Dreams: Moscow and Tehran Since the Fall of the Shah* (Washington, DC: Potomac Books, Inc., 2009), 253–254.

[2] *Persian Dreams*, 255. In late February 2005, the spent fuel return protocol was finally signed.

[3] The Rose Revolution in November 2003, the Orange Revolution in December 2004, and the Tulip Revolution in March 2005.

[4] *Persian Dreams*, 282–283.

[5] *Persian Dreams*, 260.

[6] Aleksandr Kolesnichenko, "Iran: War Is Postponed," *Argumenty i Fakty*, No. 51, December 20, 2005, CEP20051222027055.

[7] *Persian Dreams*, 303.

[8] *Persian Dreams*, 309; and ITAR–TASS, December 26, 2007, CEP20071226950142.

[9] *Persian Dreams*, 309. See also Fatemeh Teymurzadeh, "A review of Iran's defense capabilities: S–300 and increase of Iran's defense power," *Jam-e Jam Online*, January 17, 2009, IAP20090119950072.

[10] "Defense Ministry: Russia To Deliver S–300 Systems To Iran in 2008," *Agentstvo Voyennykh Novostey*, December 26, 2007, CEP20071226950195.

empire. Iran's involvement in the Tajik civil war and support for Hamas in the Palestinian territories demonstrate that theology need not be a barrier to cooperation between Shia Iran and local Sunni militants if a modus vivendi serves both sides' purposes. As one Moscow analyst put the case for handling Iran gingerly, if you are facing a hooligan, you do not break his windows because you have many windows in your own house.[176]

Despite all the concern expressed over the years in Moscow on this score, there has been scant evidence that Iran has supported the independence movement in Chechnya or the current slow-burn rebellion against Russia across the North Caucasus. One well-known Russian Middle East expert recently noted that Iran claims it is Russia's main ally against Sunni radicalism and terrorism in these regions. He stressed that there is not a single documented case of Iranian help to extremists in Russia's North Caucasus.[177] So far, Russians give generally good marks to Iranian behavior across the region ever since Tehran backed the losing side in the Tajik civil war in 1992.[178]

That the Iranians in the last two decades have not wanted to antagonize the Russians along their southern periphery is not so surprising. Iran, for example, has been the dog that has not barked in Chechnya. When the first Chechen war broke out in December 1994, Iran had already lost its gamble in Tajikistan and was in no mood to start another adventure in Russia's backyard. Moreover, the Taliban had started threatening Iranian equities in Afghanistan several months earlier.

By the time the second Chechen war broke out in August–September 1999, the Taliban had greatly extended their rule in Afghanistan. Iran now really needed Russian help there in supporting Ahmed Shah Masoud's Northern Alliance against the Taliban's effort to take over all of Afghanistan. In those circumstances, Iran was not going to upset Russia by mucking around in Chechnya, much less in those Central Asian countries adjoining Afghanistan.[179]

Besides protecting Russia from criticism over Chechnya in the Organization of the Islamic Council, Iran may have gone much further in assisting Russian efforts in Chechnya. In 1995, legendary Chechen resistance leader Shamil Basayev remarked on the lack of Iranian involvement in supporting the Chechen cause, suggesting that Iran was afraid of Russia and of course needed Russian cooperation in building a "nuclear bomb."[180]

Ten years later, in July 2006, Russia's Federal Security Service (FSB) claimed to have killed Basayev in neighboring Ingushetiya. A year later, in July 2011, an alleged direct participant in that claimed special operation asserted that the bait had been a large shipment of weapons that the FSB, Foreign Intelligence Service, Main Intelligence Directorate, and Ministry of Internal Affairs had assembled in Iran and transported through Turkey and onward into Russia's Northern Caucasus to Ingushetiya, where it was detonated as Basayev approached to inspect it.[181]

The account begs the question, never addressed in the interview, of what must have been official Iranian complicity with Russia's special services in putting together on Iranian territory the arms shipment that eventually resulted in Basayev's death. If true, it adds a layer of intriguing texture to the contradictory context in which Moscow joined other members of the UN Security Council on July 31, 2006, in approving UNSC Resolution 1696. The measure, the first in the subsequent series of half a dozen UNSC resolutions on the Iranian nuclear issue, called on Iran to suspend all enrichment-related and research and development activities by August 31, 2006, or face economic sanctions.[182]

The account of Basayev's death also suggests a payback component in Putin's decision the following year finally to visit Tehran after he and his predecessor Boris Yeltsin had politely deflected Iranian invitations for years. When Putin finally traveled to Iran in October 2007, he became the first supreme Soviet or Russian leader to visit since Joseph Stalin had attended the wartime conference there with Franklin Roosevelt and Winston Churchill in 1943.[183]

In the wake of Russia joining tough UN sanctions and breaking the S–300 contract, there were calls from Russian analysts for Russia to resurrect what they saw as its earlier constructive dialogue with Tehran on regional issues. NATO would eventually leave Afghanistan, and Hamid Karzai would not survive a day longer, they argued. What will then replace the Karzai regime? Before long, the United States and Russia will have to bring Tehran into negotiations on any framework for the future of Afghanistan, they asserted, and Iran could play a positive role in regulating the Afghan problem.[184]

At the present time, Iran probably judges that it again needs stability across this region and Russian good offices against the possibility of Taliban resurgence in Afghanistan as the United States and NATO draw down forces there. Iran may once again have to cooperate with Russia to protect its equities in the region, particularly Iran's traditional dominance in Afghanistan's western regions bordering on Iran. Russia, for its part, is quick to recognize that it has cooperated with Iran on regional issues along Russia's southern belt in the past and may need to do so again in the future should worse come to worst.

Sparring over the Caspian Sea and its immense hydrocarbon riches is an entirely different matter, however. Iran has long insisted at a minimum on a 20 percent sector of the seabed instead of the 13 to 14 percent that the more widely accepted median-line methodology would award it. In July 2001, an Iranian gunboat and military aircraft chased away two Azeri-chartered oil-exploration ships exploring for oil in the Alborz/Alof field lying outside Iran's median-line sector but within its self-declared 20 percent sector. The following year, Russia staged an impressive exercise of its Caspian Flotilla.[185]

Russia is now planning to build up to 16 new ships by 2020 and provide the Flotilla with the Bastion shore-based missile system armed with Yakhont hypersonic missiles designed to destroy surface targets at distances up to 300 kilometers. A Russian commentary on the projected fleet expansion noted that "Iran remains the only remotely feasible explanation of the sudden Russian fears in this direction."[186] Press commentary on the year's major Russian Tsentr 2011 strategic exercise speculated that the hypothetical adversary in one of the scenarios that involved the Caspian Flotilla was Iran.[187]

Middle East: Regional Calculations

In early 2011, at the onset of the Arab Spring—before the ouster of Hosni Mubarak in Egypt—the mainstream, but not official, view in Moscow on coping with rising Iranian power was: Why should we side with the United States, a country whose position in the Middle East is weakening, against Iran, a country whose position is strengthening in Iraq, Lebanon, and Syria, among others?

This attitude represented an admittedly cynical but rational calculation, even if based on the assumption, which might prove to be erroneous, of Iran as the eventual winner. Indeed, some were skeptical of the notion that Iran had gained much from the initial upheavals in the Middle East, and even suggested that Iran on balance had been a loser in the early days of the Arab Spring.[188]

As of early January 2012, the jury was still out on the impact of the Middle East upheavals on Iran's leverage in the region. Domestically, Arab-Iran differences continued to serve as barriers to any demonstration impact within Iran on the country's public, including the Green Movement. Externally, the Arab Spring in the end may prove a wash rather than a boost for Iranian stature and influence in the region.

Syria has been the latest instance of the intersection of occasionally overlapping but not identical Russian and Iranian interests in the greater Middle East. The Syrian crisis has underscored for Iran the prudence and advantages of remaining engaged with Russia. As Russia's veto of an American-backed draft resolution in October 2011 demonstrated, Russia can still wield substantial influence on outcomes in the region—in this instance prolonging diplomatic cover for Damascus to deal with the crisis on its own terms—through its retention of a veto-wielding permanent seat in the UN Security Council.[189]

Actually, Moscow and Tehran have been more rivals rather than partners for influence in Damascus, each pursuing its own goals through Bashar al-Asad's regime. For Tehran, Syria has hosted supply lines to Hizballah in Lebanon and Hamas in Gaza and taken a hardline in Arab-Israeli negotiations. For Russia, toppling Asad would threaten arms sales as well as Russia's recent investment in trying to revive Russian-Syrian ties and through them another point of entry for Russia into regional Arab-Israeli deal-making more generally. Though unintended, Russia's stance during the extended crisis has served to shelter—but cannot ultimately save—Iran's equities in Syria, a country key to Iranian influence in the region.

Putting aside the eventual impact of the Arab Spring, the standard view in Moscow—at least until the recent collapse of Iran's currency under pressure from forthcoming U.S. and EU sanctions targeting the Central Bank of Iran and imports of Iranian oil[190]—has been that Iran is a rising power that in 10 years is likely to become a power of the first rank in the Middle East and Persian Gulf. With a population of over 70 million, Iran already determines stability in the region. Thus, goes the argument, Russia cannot afford to turn Iran into an enemy and a big problem to deal with in the future.

The view among most analysts is that Moscow needs a stable and united Iran. Russia therefore needs to cooperate, not argue, with Iran. Some assert that "we" know Iran also wants good relations with "us" even though Iran does not have warm feelings toward Russia. Summing up, the view is that Iran is a great country with an ancient civilization, it is strategically located and has a lot of potential, and Russia therefore needs to engage actively with it.[191]

Some in Moscow believe Iran will relax and tone down its aggressive behavior after it acquires a nuclear bomb. However, more seem to expect that Iran will act even more belligerently. One forecast foresees Tehran heating up conflicts in Lebanon, the Gaza strip, and in parts of Iraq in order to divert attention from Iran's nuclear program.[192]

Analysts in Moscow repeat that Russia has a clear interest in avoiding and preventing a military and/or political crisis in the Middle East involving Iran. In their view, such a crisis would lead to an immediate negative reaction on the Caucasus and a wave of migration into

Azerbaijan. They fear that the fragmentation of Iran would lead to a regional catastrophe, with unmanageable refugee flows north, which one analyst puts in the 800,000 to 1 million range.[193]

Many in Moscow see a nuclear arms race in the Middle East as another threat to Russia. One military observer has written that "even if Iran and North Korea do not become Russia's enemies, in the future a missile-nuclear Iran and development of North Korea's potential can destabilize the regional and global situation and give rise to a chain reaction of proliferation (Saudi Arabia, Syria, Turkey, Egypt, Libya, Japan, South Korea, Taiwan), which also will create a danger for Russia."[194]

With a nod to the "possible" appearance of nuclear arms in the arsenals of Iran and its neighbors, none other than Russian Strategic Nuclear Forces Commander Sergei Karakayev recently warned that such a development would have grave consequences: "This may put Russia in a situation of uncontrolled use by other countries of nuclear weapons near its borders, which may lead to a real danger of our country's involvement in military conflicts of various intensity and scale."[195]

In addition, many in Russia have been expecting an American or Israeli strike against Iran for years. Since Iran's nuclear ambitions are probably unstoppable and Israel cannot accept their fulfillment, one analyst has put the chances of an Israeli strike as higher than 50 percent. In several years, this observer predicts such a strike will likely be the source of a major crisis, with the United States and Russia taking different positions. Russia would not side with Iran, but would distance itself from the United States so as not to inspire hatred toward Russia in the Muslim world.

Another analyst predicted that there would be sympathy in Russia for Israel even though Russia would officially condemn the attack. However, such an attack would only postpone the Iranian program for a few months to a year.[196] Not remarked on was the analytical tension between confidence that Iran could go forward undeterred with its missile and nuclear programs after a military attack, and fear that an attack on Iran would lead to Iran's cataclysmic fragmentation.

The Ever-present American Angle

The theme that asserts Russian policy toward Iran is just a byproduct of U.S.-Russia relations is important but frequently exaggerated.[197] Although stressed by Russian interlocutors, it does not explain everything. Whatever the state of Russia's ties with the United States at any moment, Moscow has traditionally seen good relations with Tehran as in Russia's national interests and has often bent over backwards to maintain stable relations. Conversely, though, rough patches in Moscow's ties with Washington do not automatically push Russia toward better relations with Iran. In the end, Iranian behavior frequently acts as a constraint, and in recent years

Iran's nuclear and missile programs, and rise as a power in the Middle East, have given Russia ample reasons for concern.

During Putin's years at the top since late 1999, elements of Russian-Iranian relations were inversely related to Russian-American ties from 2004–2008. Before that, though, U.S.-Russia ties were good. In December 2000, Moscow abrogated the June 1995 Gore-Chernomyrdin agreement not to sign any more arms deals with Iran and to discontinue implementing existing contracts after the end of 1999.[198] Nevertheless, Russia under Putin actually refrained from negotiating and concluding any significant new arms contracts with Iran until 2004.

Putin was the first foreign leader to reach President Bush immediately after the 9/11 attacks. The Russian leader offered to share intelligence but did not go further. However, after failing to overcome eagerness in Uzbekistan to host American forces, Putin bucked strong opposition in Moscow and made a surprising decision: to endorse American use of former Soviet airfields in Central Asia to support the effort against al Qaeda and the Taliban in Afghanistan. As for Iran, only later did Putin bother to consult with Tehran about the issue.[199]

Bush and Putin reached the high-water mark of their warm relations at the May 2002 summit in Moscow. That same year, a frustrated Iranian defense minister publicly complained that Russia did not want a strong Iran and did not want to rile the United States and was therefore not selling Iran the weapons it wanted.

However, the United States and Russia were not able to sustain the momentum of close relations. Ties began to fray over the 2003 invasion of Iraq, color revolutions in Ukraine, Georgia, and Kyrgyzstan, and U.S. encouragement of NATO membership for Georgia and Ukraine. The subsequent decline in U.S.-Russia ties bolstered those in Moscow who argued for better relations with Tehran. Nevertheless, it was not until after Iran's agreement temporarily to suspend its nuclear enrichment program and submit to an Additional Protocol that Russia began negotiations in earnest—and in secret—on the long-range S–300 and the short-range Tor-M1 air defense systems.

After these negotiations became public, Putin justified Russia's deliveries of the Tor-M1 system to Iran when he spoke at the security conference in Munich in February 2007: "Why did we do this? . . . We did this so that Iran did not feel it had been driven into a corner."[200] Russian diplomacy deftly combined continuing pressure on Iran over its nuclear program in the IAEA and UNSC with protection of Iran from even greater pressure in these same forums from the United States and other Western powers. At the same time, along a separate track,

Russia advanced its own carrot-and-stick package for Iran, largely uncoordinated with the international community.[201]

Several years later, however, with nothing to show for its efforts to slow down Tehran's nuclear program, one of Russia's first responses to "reset" with the United States in late 2008 was to put on hold the transfer of the S–300 to Iran. Ahmadinejad had exhausted his capital in Moscow by diplomacy that used Russia to gain Iran more years of progress on its nuclear enrichment program—courtesy of Russia's sheltering Iran from greater pressure.

Basically, Ahmadinejad played Putin for a fool, and in recent years it has been an open secret in Moscow that the Russian leader can no longer abide him.[202] As a result, Russia's careful coordination with Washington and the P5+1 of its current step-by-step initiative contrasts strikingly with Putin's separate bilateral 2004–2008 efforts to elicit a compromise solution from Iran on the nuclear issue.

Much, of course, is explained by the fact that the United States will always be more important to Russia than Iran. Moreover, Moscow and Washington all along have shared an interest in Iran not going nuclear despite different takes on the threat. At their summit in Washington in June 2010, Presidents Obama and Medvedev capped an impressive revival of relations that had descended to a 25-year low following the Russia-Georgia war in August 2008. Since that summit, the two sides have succeeded in sustaining positive ties despite the challenge presented by negotiations over a European missile defense system designed in part to meet the Iran threat.

Nevertheless, it is not foreordained that U.S.-Russia relations will continue on a positive trajectory or that Russian-Iranian ties will languish in a deep trough. Recent history underscores the pitfalls of such assumptions. Tehran hangs on to its Russian connection in large part in hopes that Moscow can again be a card to play in fending off further pressure from Washington and other European capitals for UNSC sanctions going beyond those of Resolution 1929. Tehran and Moscow both appear to judge that it is better to be viewed by the other as a potential card to be played than to be ignored.

Given the history of Moscow's and Tehran's dealings with each other since the advent of the Islamic Republic, the potential paradigm shift in ties that Medvedev and Putin ushered in with their support for tough sanctions and cancellation of the S–300 contract is not necessarily irreversible. Russian public opinion is drawn to American culture but put off by the exercise of American power, especially around Russian borders, and is on balance less hostile to Iran than to the United States. Moreover, mainstream expert opinion in Moscow, however much some advisors deplore Iran's nuclear and missile programs and share American goals, judges that Moscow went too far with its support for the last round of sanctions and the S–300 cut-off decision.

Moscow versus Washington: A Key Point

In general, Moscow's Iran policy accents will always differ from those of Washington even if they intersect on some major points as they do now. Even when relations are bad, Moscow seeks to engage Iran as a "neighbor" with whom all should deal diplomatically rather than threaten force, even though this engagement is frequently hollow and recognized as such by both sides.

Beyond Moscow's long-standing engagement strategy with Tehran, Russia's approach has been motivated in more recent years by its deep concerns over how the United States has wielded power as the dominant international actor since the collapse of the Soviet Union. Moscow has viewed Washington's behavior as all too often unrestrained, unconstrained, extra-legal, and excessively unilateral in using armed conflict as an instrument of choice to resolve international security issues.

Traditional Russian paranoia about the intentions of NATO and the United States began to grow when the first prospects for NATO enlargement appeared in spring 1993, and surged particularly after the March 1999 bombing of Serbia. Since then, the American invasion of Iraq in 2003, the NATO campaign over Libya in 2010, and the threat of similar action in Syria in recent months have served to stoke continuing Russian alarm.

Fundamentally, Moscow perceives all of these actions to have been against Russia's interests. Nevertheless, Moscow's concern over potential action against Iran is even more far-reaching because Iran is so close to Russia and the spillover effects of an American armed intervention would have a direct and immediate effect on Russian security interests.

Russian unilateral efforts to accommodate Iran from 2004 through 2008 made it difficult for outside analysts to perceive that, under the right conditions, Russia and the United States could work together more closely to pressure Iran. By the same token, the current differences between Russia and Iran should not obscure the potential for the two countries again to cooperate against American preferences, especially in the event of the collapse of "reset," and for Russia to do all in its power to obstruct a military campaign by Israel and/or the United States against Iran.

At this juncture, therefore, it is still too early to exclude the possibility of a fraying of Russia's commitment to tough sanctions on Iran. However, especially in the event of a deterioration of relations between Washington and Moscow, we could see a replay of the 2004–2008 dynamic of Russia extending some carrots to Iran while lending less than full support to international pressure on Tehran.

Moscow's careful coordination of step-by-step, however, so far points to a breakthrough in the other direction in Russian-Iranian relations, rather than a replay of that earlier dynamic. In opposing another round of sanctions, and even after it criticized the IAEA in November 2011 for leaking a draft report on alleged new evidence of possible military dimensions of Iran's military program, Moscow did not backtrack from its support for sanctions under UNSC Resolution 1929.[203]

Moreover, it can be speculated that there is a crocodile tears element to Russia's criticism of unilateral U.S., EU, Australian, and other national sanctions that go beyond those agreed by the UN Security Council.[204] Such criticism enables Russia to pose as a principled friend of Iran even as these non-UNSC sanctions add to the pressure on Iran. In addition, should Iran continue to defy UNSC resolutions on its nuclear enrichment program, it cannot be excluded that Russia will once again come around to supporting another round of harsher sanctions, again justifying its support with the argument "when all other options have been exhausted, why not?"[205]

Finally, Russia finds it prudent to stay engaged with Iran because of Moscow's long-standing assumption that the United States will one day return to Iran.[206] Russians are not blind to the fact that they are not held in high regard by Iranians, while Americans surprisingly still retain some popularity, more than 30 years after the Islamic revolution. When Iran and the United States reestablish ties, Russian engagement is meant to minimize the chances that Tehran will cast aside its Russia connection and leave Moscow with few equities in Iran.

In fact, there is little chance of that happening. Tehran will always want to keep a fairly robust Moscow connection, in part to balance Washington's presence and influence in the region, in part for doing business on regional issues where the interests of Iran and Russia coincide.

In Moscow, as they look to the future, Russian analysts with experience dating back to the Shah era can point out to their younger colleagues that Russia enjoyed good relations with Iran even when the United States was the dominant power there.[207] There are even veteran diplomats, such as Ambassador Nikolay Kozyrev, who served several tours in Tehran before the Islamic revolution and have vivid memories of being guests at intimate at-homes hosted by the Shah.[208]

Reacting to the November IAEA Report

For much of 2011, continuing Arab Spring developments, accelerating presidential campaigns, and the temporary slowdown in the Iranian nuclear program attributed to the Stuxnet virus led to a lull in attention to Iran.[209] That was dramatically broken in October–November by U.S. charges of an Iranian plot to kill the Saudi Ambassador Adel al-Jubeir in Washington;[210] chatter in Israel

The S–300 Contract: The Deal Unravels

From 2005–2008, negotiations with Iran on its nuclear enrichment program went nowhere. At the same time, Russian relations with the United States soured further and reached their low point in August 2008 with the Georgia-Russia war and with the U.S. announcement of a missile defense system to be based in Poland and the Czech Republic.

On November 5, 2008, in his first state of the nation speech, new Russian President Dmitriy Medvedev stated that Russia would deploy short-range Iskander missiles to Kaliningrad "to neutralize, if necessary, the missile defense system."[1]

Medvedev's statement was a bracing way to greet Barack Obama's election as U.S. President the day before. Furthermore, from all indications, the S–300 transfers to Iran were still set to go forward.[2]

However, hints soon began that Moscow was rethinking the S–300 deal. The Putin-Medvedev tandem seemed increasingly inclined to explore ways to do business with the new Obama administration. Russia was also trying to encourage Iran to agree with the P5+1 on freezing Iran's nuclear enrichment program and answering remaining questions from the IAEA.

In addition, the global financial crisis had put Putin's "energy superpower" through a severe "stress test." Several well-known Russian analysts warned of "strategic isolation" in the years ahead unless Russia cooperated closely with the United States and the West.[3]

It soon started to become clear that Moscow had decided to hold up the transfer of the S–300 to Iran despite Russia being in a state of economic shock. The price of oil—shorthand for how needy the Russian state coffers were for income in general—had plummeted to a low of $36.51/barrel on January 16, 2009, from its high of $145/barrel the previous July. Russia's gross domestic product would contract by 7.8 percent in 2009, the most of any G–20 country.

On February 4, 2009, Rosoboroneksport General Director Anatoliy Isaykin stated publicly that the S–300 contract still needed presidential approval to transfer the system to Iran.[4] Isaykin's comment was published 3 days before Vice President Joseph Biden's "reset" statement in Munich.

In mid-February, Iranian Defense Minister Najjar was back in Moscow.[5] In contrast to his December 2007 visit, when he let the cat out of the bag on the S–300 contract, this time Najjar kept silent—he apparently got nothing for his presumed efforts to urge Moscow to release the S–300s to Tehran.[6]

The S–300 Contract: The Deal Unravels (cont.)

Sources in Moscow told *Kommersant* that "Russia will not be in any hurry to start deliveries of S–300 SAM complexes to Iran inasmuch as this may hinder the nascent dialogue with the new U.S. Administration. . . . The main deterrent factor here is the opportunity for Russia's improved relations with the United States."[7]

[1] Rossiya TV, live broadcast, November 5, 2008, CEP20081105950217.

[2] On December 17, 2008, an unnamed source of RIA Novosti said that "Moscow has earlier met its obligations on supplying Tor-M1 systems to Iran and is currently implementing a contract to deliver S–300 systems." See RIA Novosti, December 17, 2008, CEP20081217950142.

[3] See, especially, Sergey Karaganov, "Amerikanskiy vyzov" [The American Challenge], *Rossiyskaya Gazeta*, October 13, 2009; Dmitri Trenin, "Russia Reborn: Reimagining Moscow's Foreign Policy," *Foreign Affairs* 88, no. 6 (November–December 2009), 64–78; and Dmitri Trenin, "U.S.-Russian Relations: How Does Russia See the Reset?" transcript of presentation and Q&A at Carnegie Endowment for International Peace, Washington, DC, October 28, 2009, available at <http://carnegieendowment.org/files/Full_Transcript%20of%20Event.pdf>.

[4] Interview of Rosoboroneksport General Director Anatoliy Isaykin by Vadim Soloyev, "Rosoboroneksport Strengthens Positions," *Nezavisimaya Gazeta*, February 4, 2009, CEP20090205557001.

[5] "Russia's Position on S–300 Air Defense Systems to Iran Unlikely to Change," *Interfax–AVN Online*, February 17, 2009, CEP20090217950042.

[6] "Delivery of S–300 Air Defense Systems to Iran Could Be Postponed," *Interfax–AVN Online*, March 10, 2009, CEP20090310950172; Philip P. Pan and Karen DeYoung, "Russia Signaling Interest in Deal On Iran, Analysts Say," *The Washington Post*, March 18, 2009; Dmitriy Litovkin, "Iran's Waiting for the Russian SAM Launchers Finally Ended; But So Far They Still Have No Missiles," *Izvestiya*, March 18, 2009, CEP20090320358009; "Russia says not supplying S–300 missiles to Iran, source says contract in place," RIA Novosti, March 18, 2009, CEP20090318950284.

[7] Yelena Kupriyanova report: "Russia-Iran: At Military Department Level," *SMI.ru*, February 17, 2009, CEP20090219358003.

about the impending need for a military strike against Iran's nuclear program;[211] a U.S. campaign to increase sanctions and pressure on Iran by urging the IAEA to release evidence suggesting that Iran had been working on technologies for designing and detonating a nuclear device;[212] publication by the IAEA of this evidence;[213] a massive explosion at a missile base 30 miles from Tehran that killed General Hassan Tehrani Moghaddam, founder of Iran's missile program, and 16 others;[214] a tough IAEA Board of Governors resolution castigating Iran for continuing to defy its obligations under IAEA Board of Governors and UN Security Council resolutions;[215] subsequent additional sanctions imposed by the United States, Britain, Canada, and France;[216] the Iranian sacking of the British embassy in Tehran;[217] and additional sanctions levied by the European Union.[218]

Official Moscow did not come to Iran's defense on the plot charge, but also did not join its voice to Washington's.[219] However, following the leak of the November 8 IAEA report on Iran, Moscow's furious reaction over the early release, contents, and spin given the report was no mere bargaining ploy but reflected genuine annoyance and some real anger. Although Medvedev, a year earlier, had noted that "It is obvious that Iran is coming close to the possession of potential that could in principle be used to create nuclear weapons," the Foreign Ministry now put out a statement charging that the IAEA was "juggling with information in order to create an impression that the Iranian nuclear program allegedly has a military component." The statement suggested that the campaign surrounding the report was aimed at undermining Moscow's lead on step-by-step. It claimed recent movement by Iran toward the IAEA and criticized the IAEA report for not mentioning it.[220]

Most Russian experts did not have to be persuaded that Iran had been engaged in a military nuclear program for some years but did not believe the IAEA report presented serious new grounds for imposing another round of sanctions against Iran.[221] One Russian analyst, Vladimir Yevseyev, called the Western spin given the IAEA report a "provocation" that was aimed at confronting Russia with the choice of either supporting more UNSC sanctions or countenancing an Israeli strike on Iran.[222]

After all the pressure on it to compromise and support additional sanctions, Moscow was pleased with the P5+1 decision not to go forward with another sanctions draft in November. At the IAEA Board of Governors meeting, Russia praised the official resolution, which took Iran to task for its failure to cooperate in resolving questions about its nuclear program, including "the existence of possible military dimensions," while also including a reference to October 30 and November 3, 2011, letters from Iran to the IAEA director general expressing Iran's "readiness to cooperate with the Agency."[223]

Russia called the sacking of the British embassy in Tehran "unacceptable" and deserving of "condemnation."[224] But Russia also criticized the additional sanctions declared around this time by its P5+1 partners and other countries.[225] Foreign Ministry spokesman Aleksandr Lukashevich warned that unilateral sanctions and threats of force were "fraught with the gravest consequences" and threatened to wreck Tehran's cooperation with the IAEA.[226]

While Moscow will not defend Tehran's nuclear enrichment program, it also will not join efforts to isolate Iran. In the middle of Russia's furious reaction to the release of the November 8 IAEA report on Iran, a representative of Russia's Security Council signed a vague strategic cooperation agreement with his counterpart from Iran's Supreme National Security Council, visiting Moscow.[227] Even some of Ahmadinejad's harshest critics, such as Larijani, called for promoting Iran's relations with Russia "to the highest level."[228] Moreover, if Iran eventually does respond productively to step-by-step, Moscow's initiative could change the mix and lead to a new Russo-Iranian rapprochement regarding the nuclear issue.

However, not even Moscow seems optimistic that, beyond engagement for the sake of engagement, step-by-step will alter anything until after the changing of the presidential guard in Tehran. But some change *is* inevitable as the Iranian program recovers from its recent setbacks,

Would Russia Welcome Military Action Against Iran?

Over the years, there has been speculation that Russia would welcome an outside attack on Iran because it would lead to a dramatic spike in world oil prices and perhaps "solve" the Iranian nuclear issue at the same time.[1] Indeed, many Russian analysts have been expecting an Israeli strike for years and some regard it as likely since Iran's nuclear ambitions are probably unstoppable and Israel cannot accept their fulfillment. Many in Moscow would probably privately sympathize with such an attack while publicly condemning it. Russia would not side with Iran, but would distance itself from U.S. support for Israel so as not to inspire hatred toward Russia in the Muslim world.[2]

Tension in the Middle East in fact does contribute to keeping the price of oil high. However, contrary to the reported sympathy for a potential Israeli strike, since the beginning of UN Security Council deliberations on the Iranian nuclear issue in 2006, Moscow has bargained hard and prevailed in insisting that all decisions exclude any hint of a UN Charter Chapter VII, Article 42, threat of force.[3] In the view of analysts in Moscow, an Israeli strike could not put an end to the Iranian nuclear program but would certainly lead Iran to abandon the NPT. Moreover, there would be unforeseen consequences ranging from a regional war to a regional nuclear arms race.[4]

To Moscow's frustration and regret, Russia's help to Iran in the UN Security Council has not deterred Iran from inviting a possible armed strike by continuing to move ahead with its nuclear and missile programs. In October–November 2011, Moscow appeared more concerned than ever over the possibility of an Israeli strike on Iran. Foreign Minister Lavrov warned that any armed strike against Iran would be "a very grave mistake fraught with unpredictable consequences."[5] President Medvedev stated that an attack would be "a disaster for the Middle East" and called on all "to exhale, to calm down."[6]

When Deputy Foreign Minister Sergei Ryabkov traveled to Israel at the end of November, he cautioned that any attack on Iran would result in "a significant increase in risks to Israel's national security." Ryabkov asserted that "Iran has no right to have a nuclear bomb" but conceded that it was "obviously . . . making progress in its nuclear program." Nevertheless, Ryabkov warned that Russia would "try to prevent, by all means," any attempt to attack Iran.[7]

Two weeks later, a story in the Russian press reported that Russian "preparations to minimize the losses from possible military operations against Tehran" had begun more than a year earlier. A military analyst cited in the article did not rule out that if Tehran were "threatened with total military defeat in the event of resistance to a ground invasion of Iran by U.S. and NATO troops, Russia will supply military assistance. At least at the military-technical level."[8]

Whether true or not, the remark was an entirely new element in recent Russian discourse and another sign of concern in Moscow over the possibility of an attack on Iran. Although the analyst may have been offering mere personal speculation, it cannot be ruled out that his comment was perhaps intended to inject a hypothetical complication in suspected Israeli and U.S. war plans. Logically, moreover, it suggested at least one scenario under which Russia would walk away from some of its obligations not to supply a wide array of weapons to Iran under UNSC Resolution 1929.

Were Moscow actually to give military assistance to Iran in such an eventuality, Russia would be going beyond its obligations under the 2001 Russia-Iran Treaty signed by then Presidents Mohammad Khatami and Vladimir Putin in Moscow. That treaty does not commit either side to render military aid to the other in case of aggression by a third party, but merely "not to give any help to the aggressor" and to assist a settlement on the basis of the UN Charter and international law.[9]

[1] Most recently, a very high-ranking Russian official reportedly told a European head of state that "We will not shed a tear if the nuclear sites are attacked. Israel will not permit Iran to obtain nuclear weapons." The European interlocutor reportedly attributed the Russian official's comments to the impact that such an attack would have on driving up the price of oil and making Iran more dependent on Russia for nuclear program spare parts; see Eli Bardenstein, Amit Kohen, and Gid'on Kouts, "Russia's Double Game," *Ma'ariv,* November 7, 2011, GMP20111107735008.

[2] Author's conversations in Moscow, May 2010.

[3] The matter of ruling out the threat of force against Iran is an old issue for Russia. Russia does not have a problem with putting more pressure on Iran, as long as it is twinned with engagement and not the threat of force and isolation. When the UNSC passed its first resolution on the Iranian nuclear program, Moscow made sure it excluded any Chapter VII, Article 42, threat of force (John W. Parker, *Persian Dreams: Moscow and Tehran Since the Fall of the Shah* [Washington, DC: Potomac Books, Inc., 2009], 250 and 270). Russia has been consisted on this point over the years, and all the subsequent resolutions on Iran have been bounded by the original resolution's noninvocation of Article 42.

[4] "Russian Pundits Comment on IAEA Report on Iran's Nuclear Program," RIA Novosti, November 9, 2011, CEP20111109950158; Nikolay Pakhomov, "The IAEA Report: Without Sensations and Consequences," *Politkom.ru,* November 11, 2011, CEP20111111004017; and Vladimir Yevseyev, "Psychological intimidation of Iran will lead to a new war," RIA Novosti, November 15, 2011, available at <http://en.rian.ru/analysis/20111115/168714032.html>.

[5] "Hostilities against Iran would have unpredictable consequences—Lavrov (Part 2)," *Interfax–AVN Online,* November 7, 2011, CEP20111107950060.

[6] "Russia's Medvedev warns that Israel's 'threats' to Iran may lead to 'big war,'" Rossiya 1, November 8, 2011, CEP20111108950084.

[7] Eli Bradenstein, interview with Russian Deputy Foreign Minister Sergei Ryabkov, "Any Act of Terror is Unjustified," *Ma'ariv,* December 1, 2011, GMP20111201736006.

[8] Sergey Konovalov, "Moscow Optimizes Military Grouping in South. Russia Is Preparing an Appropriate Response to

Would Russia Welcome Military Action Against Iran? (cont.)

Possible Strikes by Tel Aviv and Washington Against Tehran," *Nezavisimoye Voyennoye Obozreniye Online*, December 15, 2011, CEP20111215358007. The military analyst is identified as Colonel Vladimir Popov.

⁹ Mikhail Kalmykov, "Russia, Iran sign relations and cooperation treaty," ITAR–TASS, March 12, 2001, CEP20010312000191. For context, see *Persian Dreams*, 208–211. For the full text of the treaty, see <www.lawrussia.ru/texts/legal_523/doc523a391x473.htm>.

international sanctions bite deeper, elections take place, and Iran's new post-Ahmadinejad leaders decide what to do next.

Will Putin Change Policy?

Much in Russia-Iran relations will depend on policy choices in Moscow, Tehran, and Washington in the years ahead, and these choices are by no means foreordained. Forecasting future relations cannot be based on a straight line from present trends. Besides presidential elections in Russia in March 2012, voters will go to the polls in the United States in November 2012 and in Iran in summer 2013.

Only in Russia, where Putin and Medvedev revealed on September 24, 2011, that the two men had decided between themselves to trade jobs and that Putin's name would be on the ballot for a third term, are the elections all but foreordained. The announcement made clear their disdain for truly democratic elections, as well as their presumption that the Russian public would put up with it. In fact, a joke making the rounds soon after illustrated the Russian public's cynical but still passive amusement over the development: "February 2012. Polling place poster: On Sunday 4 March elections will be held for president of the Russian Federation V.V. Putin."

However, that submissiveness soon changed. When fans booed Putin after a martial arts boxing match in Moscow on November 21, it was a harbinger of greater things to come.[229] Widely documented instances of fraud during the Duma elections of December 4 provoked active disgust among many Russians, particularly net-savvy young urban professionals. Analysis would suggest that the regime stole some 14 million votes in barely winning a majority of Duma seats, down sharply from its earlier two-thirds majority.[230] The demonstrations that followed—the largest since those preceding the collapse of the Soviet Union—quickly threatened to undermine the legitimacy of Putin's rule.

There were some parallels between these protests and those by the Green Movement in Iran after that country's fraudulent presidential elections in June 2009. To its credit, however, after initial stumbles, including the arrest of blogosphere anticorruption activist and opposition leader

Aleksey Navalny and 300 others during the first antielectoral fraud demonstration of some 5,000 people on December 5, the Putin regime chose to eschew a brutal response. Instead, it moved quickly to try to take the wind out of the sails of the Russian protest movement through hardball though still peaceful means aimed at defending itself and preparing for a political counterattack.

Some of these initiatives on balance probably worked. They included encouragement of the candidacy of businessman Mikhail Prokhorov on the March ballot, hints of electoral reform down the road—without overturning the official results of the Duma elections of December 4—and the reshuffling of some key personnel. Other gestures, even while credible to many Russians, provoked the scorn of those already ready to join the protests. These included Putin's claims that demonstrators had been paid to show up and suggestions that Washington was orchestrating the demonstrations.[231]

On balance, even after the mass demonstrations in cities across Russia on December 10 and 24—some 50,000 and 120,000 in Moscow, respectively—the upcoming presidential balloting still appears to be Putin's to lose.[232] However, Navalny has set out to organize mass demonstrations— starting with 1 million protestors across Russia in February, then 2 million—with the aim of annulling the Duma elections of December 4, preventing Putin from winning outright on March 4 and forcing him into a second round, and rewriting the rules for presidential elections.[233]

As Iran has watched these developments unfold, official Tehran has probably been hoping that Putin will prevail. During Medvedev's presidency, there was speculation in Moscow that Tehran favored Putin, seeing hope for reviving closer ties in his return to the presidency.[234] In fact, there was some basis for this speculation. In June 2010, a hardline conservative daily affiliated with the Islamic Revolution Guards Corps commented on Russian *Newsweek*'s "leak" of a draft foreign policy document. The commentary saw in the disclosure signs of a coup by Medvedev and his circle against Putin and his team. According to the Iranian publication, Putin's approach attributed to "countries like Iran . . . an important role in the confrontation between Moscow and the West." However, the commentary complained that Medvedev was now calling for strengthening relations with America and Europe in order to help modernize Russia's economy, and for joining them in pushing a tough sanctions resolution through the UN Security Council.[235]

It is unlikely that Putin and Medvedev have differed on the substance of policy toward Iran. Putin definitely is more invested in relations with Tehran given his close involvement in pursuing bilateral ties with Iran for 8 years while president. Nevertheless, he also has more reason to be bitter over Tehran's lack of responsiveness to Russian efforts to find face-saving solutions to the nuclear issue while he was president, and since. It is widely understood among Iran-watchers in Moscow that neither Putin nor Medvedev can stand Ahmadinejad. Buttressing that view, it was Putin who, in June 2010, just after passage of UNSC Resolution 1929, reportedly stressed to Sarkozy that the S–300s would not be going to Iran.[236]

Nevertheless, while clear about his displeasure with Tehran's behavior, Putin has often been more measured than Medvedev in his public statements. In December 2010, for example, parsing his words carefully, Putin told CNN's Larry King that Russia shared with the IAEA a desire for "exhaustive answers" from Iran on its nuclear program. "At the same time," he said, "we have no grounds for suspecting Iran of seeking to possess nuclear weapons."[237]

Medvedev, in contrast, has been far more blunt and less willing to hide his lack of sympathy with Tehran's behavior, especially since it became all the more egregious on his presidential watch. In July 2010, it was Medvedev who pointedly stated that "It is obvious that Iran is coming close to the possession of potential that could in principle be used to create nuclear weapons."[238] Earlier, after the discovery of Iran's hidden facility at Fordow, Medvedev called on Iran to "present convincing evidence of its intention to strive for the development of nuclear energy strictly for peaceful aims."[239]

Consistent with this bluntness was Medvedev's public embracing of the S–300 cut-off. Putin also, as we have seen, supported the decision. Breaking the contract meant giving up an issue of continuing leverage, but also irritation, in bilateral U.S.-Russia relations. In giving up this Iran card in October 2010, even as polls predicted significant losses in midterm elections for the Obama administration, the Putin-Medvedev tandem in effect demonstrated its commitment to continuing to work on Iran with the American President regardless of the outcome of the U.S. midterm elections.

However, a telephone-menu joke making the rounds during Medvedev's presidency made it plain that Putin has been and will remain boss: "Hello, you have dialed the office of the president of the Russian Federation. If you would like to speak with Dmitriy Anatolyevich Medvedev, please press number 2." Given Putin's long track record as dominant leader and his frequent jibes at Washington, it would be a mistake in divining future Russian policy to attribute to Putin a reflexive and inflexible anti-Americanism. In reality, he has been far more calculating and sometimes even subtle. "The style will change," according to Fedor Lukyanov, editor of *Russia in Global Affairs*. "It will become more confrontational, but this does not mean a change of course."[240] As one expert on civil-military issues put it last summer, Putin often talks meat-eater but acts vegetarian, which seems true regarding the United States but not on other issues such as Chechnya and Georgia.[241]

Looking forward, even before December's mass demonstrations against Putin, some observers predicted that the next Russian president will preside over a period of tough economic and social reforms from 2012–2015.[242] Since the global financial crisis of 2008–2009, Russia's growth rate has recovered to about 4 percent, but that rate may not be sustainable.[243]

In any event, 4 percent is still far from the 7 percent averaged from 1999 through 2007, and the 6.5 percent that Putin has called for in order for Russia to attain fifth place among the world's leading economies.[244]

Corruption remains rampant. Capital flight has not been staunched: net outflow more than doubled in 2011 to an estimated $70 billion (or even $85 billion), well above the $34 billion estimated in 2010.[245] The brain drain stands at around 50,000 per year and climbing, with those leaving three times more likely to be highly educated than those who stay.[246]

Demographic projections for Russia's 140-million-plus population remain grim: Nikolay Patrushev, secretary of the Security Council, warns that the country's working age population will decrease by at least 10 million between now and 2025 and that "everywhere we are confronting an acute shortage of skilled personnel," even more severely in Russia's thinly populated Far East.[247] Public health care and education continue to decline. Former Finance Minister Aleksey Kudrin has continued to warn since his dismissal that "increasing military spending in Russia threatens an increase in the support for health care and education programs."[248] Promised higher pensions and military expenditures will be impossible to sustain without sustained high oil prices. Putin may be able to temporize in the short run given predictions that oil will average from $100 to $120 a barrel in 2012.[249] Yet prices at the end of 2011 were below $117 a barrel, the price that is needed for the 2012 budget to balance.[250]

Russian defense expert Ruslan Pukhov estimates that Russia would have to spend annually more than 4 percent of its gross domestic product for the next 10 years to make up for 20 years of "underfunding, neglect and degradation in the military." Yet Pukhov warns that more than 1 to 2 years of spending at that level on military modernization would mean that "we can forget about modernizing the rest of the country."[251]

No wonder that even Putin on one occasion last fall referred to the "bitter pills" that Russians will have to swallow when the government begins to tackle the country's economic challenges and choices in the period ahead.[252] Putin's phrase suggested to some that he will have to return to the reform program that he abandoned in 2003–2004—as the price of oil rose and he accelerated a campaign to rein in the oligarchs by imprisoning politically ambitious Yukos head Mikhail Khodorkovsky—if he hopes to pull Russia out of its current economic stall.[253]

Putin has always been capable of surprises. His regime has reacted grudgingly yet more nimbly than might have been expected to the protests against the conduct of the Duma elections of December 2011. His own experts have warned him that, without radical changes, Russia's economic growth will wane, setting the stage for an unavoidable crisis in the last half of this decade.[254]

However, we will not know whether Putin intends to dig in and risk stagnation or move forward on economic and political reforms until after the upcoming presidential elections in March. Either way, but especially if he tries to hunker down and defend his regime rather than try to transform it, questions of his legitimacy and responsibility for Russia's mismanagement are likely to grow rather than diminish as Russia confronts its systemic shortcomings, and as pressure mounts for change in the coming months and years.

On foreign policy, at least, the evidence so far suggests that Putin has not lost the ability for cold calculation that more often than not trumps his worst instincts. Under any rational scenario, Moscow would benefit from a sustained period of external peace and calm given the fundamental economic, social, and political problems it faces at home. All of these factors taken together would normally be a disincentive to stirring things up with the United States by unnecessarily making common cause with an Iran that continues to advance its military nuclear and missile programs. To them must now be added Putin's ongoing efforts to restore his legitimacy and avoid marginalization by a public that increasingly sees him as the problem and not the solution to Russia's domestic problems.

Although now seemingly deadlocked, Washington and Moscow presumably will continue intensive negotiations over the contours of possible cooperation on missile defense in Europe. The Russian presidential "campaign," with elections set for March 4 and inauguration for May 7, will coincide with the runup to the May 20–21, 2012, NATO summit in Chicago. The atmospherics of U.S.-Russia relations in the months ahead will depend substantially on how Moscow decides to handle its differences with Washington and NATO on missile defense.

The signs so far suggest that Russia will opt for continuing dialogue despite some fundamental differences, and choose a military response far short of a new arms race. In October, Kremlin foreign policy aide Sergey Prikhodko denied that differences over missile defense and the so-called Magnitskiy List were leading to a cooling in ties.[255] In November, Medvedev outlined Russia's military response, but he let it be known several days earlier that Moscow would "not close the way to the discussion of the situation with the missile defense systems in Europe with our partners in NATO."[256]

Dmitriy Rogozin, Russia's envoy to NATO until December 2011, hinted last fall that Moscow would engage in brinksmanship on whether Putin would agree to a Russia–NATO Council summit, which he linked to a compromise on missile defense, on the margins of NATO's summit in Chicago in May.[257] But Russia already has enough on its plate to discourage it from manufacturing an unnecessary crisis over missile defense.[258] Moreover, it will be hard for Putin to skip the summit with NATO if he is already in Chicago for the G–8 summit that will precede it. Given what will probably be a rising need to bolster his legitimacy at home, Putin would profit by being seen in the company of other world leaders chosen by fair elections. Finally, Putin can only give substance to Moscow's emphasis on the need for continued dialogue by showing up in Chicago and engaging NATO leaders on the subject.

However, should Moscow all the same decide on acrimonious exchanges with Washington on missile defense, and Putin risk being uninvited to the Chicago G–8 summit by stealing the March 4 elections and provoking more protests at home, he may well strike a tougher tone on relations with Washington more generally. He does, after all, have a long paper trail of venomous digs at the United States.[259]

Putin seems sure to adopt sharper elbows on the Middle East. The one foreign policy issue on which he appeared to disagree with Medvedev was Russia's abstention on UNSC Resolution 1973 on Libya in March 2011. According to some, Putin decided against Medvedev's reelection as president after the two appeared publicly to clash over the abstention decision.[260] Beyond Libya, Putin could use policy toward Iran to flaunt Moscow's independence from Washington, but there are plenty of other issues he could pick to inflate the appearance of Russian distance from the United States.[261]

Syria is a more likely candidate. Putin is already deeply distrustful of American or other Western efforts to secure Security Council approval for what might be in any way interpreted as a green or even amber light for military interference in Syria. U.S. and Western pressure on Syria's Bashar al-Asad regime is now beginning to be tacked on to the litany of U.S. and NATO perfidy in twisting UNSC decisions beginning with the bombing of Yugoslavia in 1999 and running through the invasion of Iraq in 2003 and the campaign against Libya's Qadhafi in 2011.

Russia vetoed the U.S.-backed UNSC draft resolution of October 4, 2011, and has continued to urge on other powers its self-described more balanced approach toward the Asad regime in Damascus and its opponents.[262] A commentary in the government daily *Rossiyskaya Gazeta* after the UNSC vote asserted that the veto of the Syria resolution, even though Asad opponents were burning Russian flags, had shown that Russia would not be a "yes-man" to American policy and that Washington would "have to reckon" with Moscow's opinion.[263]

As for Iran, Putin would not likely want to go too far in backtracking on Russia's current approach should Iran continue to thumb its nose at Security Council resolutions on the nuclear issue. Moreover, Moscow's vote for UNSC Resolution 1929, Medvedev's tough implementation decree, and Russia's S–300 contract cancellation give Moscow little—though not insurmountable—room for retreat on arms sales to Iran in the absence of a change in Iranian behavior.

However, the probability of Putin's paring back these decisions will rise in the event that President Obama is not reelected or gives "reset" short shift in his second term, or in the event

Moscow perceives grave threats to Tehran's security and moves to bolster Iran's defenses. Nevertheless, absent such a perceived threat, and given his past experiences with Iran, Putin would move toward Tehran only to reciprocate Iranian steps toward a more cooperative relationship with IAEA inspectors.

Notes

[1] Laurence Kelly, *Diplomacy and Murder in Tehran: Alexander Griboyedov and Imperial Russia's Mission to the Shah of Persia* (London: Tauris Parke, 2006), 195–202.

[2] ITAR–TASS, December 26, 2007, CEP20071226950142 (Open Source Center product number); and John W. Parker, *Persian Dreams: Moscow and Tehran Since the Fall of the Shah* (Washington, DC: Potomac Books, Inc., 2009), 309. There were several detailed accounts in the Russian media of negotiations over the system going back to 2004. See *Persian Dreams*, 309; and also Fatemeh Teymurzadeh, "A review of Iran's defense capabilities: S–300 and increase of Iran's defense power," *Jam-e Jam Online*, January 17, 2009, IAP20090119950072.

[3] Konstantin Lantratov and Alexandra Gritskova, "Iran Shields Its Nuclear Activities by Russian Missiles," *Kommersant.com*, December 26, 2007, CEP20071226950405; and Ilya Azar, "Axis of Evil–300," *Gazeta.ru*, December 26, 2007, CEP20071227018005.

[4] Aleksandr Babakin and Vladimir Ivanov, "Bombshell for Greater Middle East? Delivery of Surface-to-Air Missile Systems to Iran Threatens to Have Explosive Consequences," *Nezavisimoye Voyennoye Obozreniye*, December 9, 2005, CEP20051209436002; and "Russia: Defense Ministry Source Says to Honor Tor-M1 Supply Contract with Iran," ITAR-TASS, December 23, 2005, CEP20051223027061.

[5] Yakovina Ivan and Ilya Kramnik, "Superiority Complex. Russia Prepared to Give Iran the Chance Not to Be Intimidated by United States," *Lenta.ru*, December 27, 2007, CEP20071228358004.

[6] Thom Shanker and Nicholas Kulish, "U.S. and Poland Set Missile Deal," *The New York Times*, August 15, 2008.

[7] "Iran Says Delivery Date of S–300 Missiles Goes Back to 2008," Iranian Students News Agency, October 11, 2010, IAP20101011950008.

[8] Lieutenant-General Leonid Sazhin, quoted in "Iran could have had S–300 years ago if it had agreed on price—Russian expert," ITAR–TASS, October 21, 2010, CEP20101021950244.

[9] Steven Erlanger and Elaine Sciolino, "Bush Says Iran Spurns New Offer on Uranium," *The New York Times*, June 15, 2008. For texts of the letter and the attachment updating the P5+1's June 2006 proposal, see "Iran Nuclear: Joint Letter," London, Foreign & Commonwealth Office, June 14, 2008, EUP20080615167003.

[10] For developments across the board up to May 2008, see *Persian Dreams*, passim. On the joint venture offer, see 258–263. Putin may subsequently have elaborated on this offer when he visited Tehran in October 2007, 306.

[11] Neil MacFarquhar, "Security Council Presses Iran on Nuclear Program," *The New York Times*, September 28, 2008. From 2006 to 2010, Russia has approved six UNSC resolutions critical of Iran: UNSC Resolution 1696 of July 31, 2006; 1737 of December 23, 2006; 1747 of March 24, 2007; 1803 of March 3, 2008; 1835 of September 27, 2008; and 1929 of June 9, 2010. The first had invoked Chapter VII, Articles 40 and 41 of the UN Charter, but Russia had made sure it did not implicitly or explicitly mention Article 42, the only article under which the use of force against Iran could have been authorized. All the subsequent resolutions have been bounded by the original resolution's noninvocation of Article 42. See *Persian Dreams*, 270 and 289.

[12] Viktor Litovkin, executive editor of the *Nezavisimoye Voyennoye Obozreniye* military magazine, told Ekho Moskvy Radio that "The fact that we have a contract with Iran on the supply of S–300PMU–1 is also an open secret. Such a contract exists. Another question is that because of some political motives we are not currently supplying [it] or we have not yet managed to produce this battalion [Russian division] or two battalions of these air defense missile systems and therefore we cannot supply [them]." Ekho Moskvy Radio, December 22, 2008, CEP20081222950246.

[13] Brian Knowlton with Peter Baker and John M. Broder, "Obama Warns of Further Economic Pain," *The New York Times*, December 8, 2008.

[14] Interview of Rosoboroneksport General Director Anatoliy Isaykin by Vadim Soloyev, "Rosoboroneksport Strengthens Positions," *Nezavisimaya Gazeta*, February 4, 2009, CEP20090205557001.

[15] The Shanghai Cooperation Organization (SCO) evolved from post-Soviet border negotiations between China and Russia, Kazakhstan, Kyrgyzstan, and Tajikistan. Together with Uzbekistan, they established the SCO in June 2001. In 2004, the SCO granted Mongolia observer status, followed by India, Iran, and Pakistan in 2005.

[16] "Acrobatic Diplomacy," editorial report, *Gazeta.ru*, June 16, 2009, CEP20090617015001.

[17] "Ahmadinejad's visit to Russia signals development of Russian-Iranian relations in future," Interfax, June 16, 2009, CEP20090616964057.

[18] Nazila Fathi, "In a Death Seen Around the World, a Symbol of Iranian Protests," *The New York Times*, June 23, 2009.

[19] "Moscow Concerned Over Use of Force, Death of Civilians in Iran," *Interfax–AVN Online*, June 26, 2009, CEP20090626950139. This was a far cry from American reaction. Several days earlier, President Barack Obama had said that "The United States and the international community have been appalled and outraged by the threats, the beatings and imprisonments of the last few days. I strongly condemn these unjust actions, and I join with the American people in mourning each and every innocent life that is lost." Glenn Kessler, "Obama Sharpens Criticism of Iran," *The Washington Post,* June 24, 2009.

[20] Ali Akbar Hashemi Rafsanjani, now head of the Expedience Council and the Assembly of Experts, told the crowd that many had doubts about the June 12 vote and "we should work to address those doubts." Robert F. Worth, "Tehran Losing Iranians' Trust, Ex-Leader Says," *The New York Times*, July 18, 2009.

[21] Patrick Clawson, "Much Traction from Measured Steps: The Iranian Opposition, the Nuclear Issue, and the West," Policy Focus #100, The Washington Institute for Near East Policy, January 2010, 5–6.

[22] An article in the reformist *E'temad*, for example, asserted, "Iranians are so distrustful of Russia, that they say that the Kremlin will make a deal with the United States over Iran's nuclear program, and will join the Western camp. With its support of the four resolutions of the UN Security Council's sanctions against Iran, Russia has proved that the Iranians' assumption is not too far from reality. The Russians are known for their political games, and for jumping from one branch to another in their diplomacy, and Iran's public opinion cannot believe in the goodwill of such politicians." See Mehdi Tajik, "Neither Russian Aircraft, nor Russian Pilots," *E'temad*, July 27, 2009, IAP20090730950085. Another critique of the president's "Look East" policy complained that "What in truth is strange and irrational is the diplomatic conduct of the Ahmadinejad government. It is not clear why and by which criteria

it has cast all its eggs into the basket of Russia and China and restricted its freedom of action in the international sphere." See Davud Hermidas-Bavand, "Useless Game," *E'temad Online*, July 28, 2009, IAP20090729950159. See also Farzaneh Rusta'i, "Russians Swindle Friends Heavily," *E'temad*, August 12, 2009, IAP20090829950039; Elaheh Kula'i, "Iran, Russia and the West," *E'temad Online*, August 23, 2009, IAP20090823950058; and editorial by editor-in-chief, "Basket in Hand, or Sincere Messenger?" *Aftab-e Yazd*, August 29, 2009, IAP20090901950115.

[23] "Moscow's Unsuccessful Stake on Ahmadinezhad," *Nezavisimaya Gazeta Online*, August 6, 2009, CEP20090806025007. On specific stakeholders in trade with Iran, the editorial stated, "According to official data, Russian-Iranian trade turnover has registered an upward trend since the year 2000, and the volume has increased more than fivefold. Turnover in 2008 increased by 12.1 percent in comparison with 2007. Although the figures for the volume of trade last year were relatively modest—$3.7 billion— it is known that a number of major Russian enterprises implementing contracts with Iran have a direct interest in the development of ties with the Islamic Republic. These are, specifically, the Rosoboroneksport [Rosoboronexport] Federal State Unitary Enterprise, the Megafon, KamAZ, and Obyedinennaya Aviastroitelnaya Korporatsiya [Amalgamated Aircraft Manufacturing Corporation] Open Joint-Stock Companies, and the Atomstroyeksport Closed joint-Stock Company and Gazprom."

[24] Hasan Ganji, "Why Down With Russia?" *Javan,* November 3, 2009, IAP20091211011003; and Hoseyn Shari'atmadari, ". . . and now, tomorrow's demonstrations," *Keyhan*, November 3, 2009, IAP20091103950119.

[25] "YouTube Clip Shows Iranian Protesters Chanting 'Death to Russia,'" *YouTube.com*, February 11, 2010, IAP20100211950098.

[26] Robert F. Worth and Nazila Fathi, "Police Are Said to Have Killed 10 in Iran Protests," *The New York Times,* December 28, 2009; Michael Slackman, "Arrests by Iran Are a Bid to Quell Wide Protests," *The New York Times*, February 10, 2010; and Thomas Erdbrink and Glenn Kessler, "Iran Is 'Nuclear State,' Ahmadinejad Says," *The Washington Post*, February 12, 2010. For an analysis of the security forces arrayed against the Green Movement, see Hossein Aryan, "Iran's Green Movement in the Doldrums?" Radio Free Europe/Radio Liberty, April 26, 2010, available at <www.rferl.org/articleprint-view/2024935.html>.

[27] Ye. V. Dunaeva, "Rossiysko-Iranskiye Otnosheniya—Vzglyad iz Tegerana" [Russian-Iranian Relations—The View from Teheran], April 29, 2010, available at <www.iimes.ru/rus/frame_stat.html>.

[28] The Qom crisis began on Monday, September 21, when Iran gave the IAEA a note declaring a small "pilot" nuclear facility. IAEA officials on Tuesday, September 22, informed the United States. See Karen DeYoung and Michael D. Shear, "U.S., Allies Say Iran Has Secret Nuclear Facility," *The Washington Post,* September 26, 2009; David E. Sanger and William J. Broad, "U.S. and Allies Press Iran Over Nuclear Plant 'Deception,'" *The New York Times*, September 26, 2009; and Helene Cooper and Mark Mazzetti, "A Cryptic Note From Tehran Ignites Days of Urgent Diplomacy," *The New York Times*, September 26, 2009.

[29] "Medvedev Issues Special Statement on Iran's Nuclear Program," ITAR–TASS, September 25, 2009, CEP20090925950315.

[30] Steven Erlanger and Mark Landler, "Iran Agrees to Send Enriched Uranium To Russia," *The New York Times*, October 2, 2009; Glenn Kessler, "Iran, Major Powers Reach Agreement On Series of

Points," *The Washington Post*, October 2, 2009; Glenn Kessler, "Iran Seeks Deal For Reactor. U.S. Sees Diplomatic Benefit in Helping Medical Treatment," *The Washington Post*, October 11, 2009; Massimo Calabresi, "Obama's Secret Iran Talks: Setting the Stage for a Deal?" *Time*, November 2, 2009; and International Institute for Strategic Studies, "The Iranian Nuclear Crisis," *Strategic Comments* 15, no. 8, October 2009, available at <www.iiss.org/publications/strategic-comments/past-issues/volume-15-2009/volume-15-issue-8/the-iranian-nuclear-crisis/>.

[31] David E. Sanger, "Tentative Accord Would Slow Iran in Building Nuclear Bomb," *The New York Times*, October 22, 2009; and Glenn Kessler, "Iranian Officials Accept Draft Deal on Uranium Transfer," *The Washington Post*, October 22, 2009.

[32] "Ahmadinejad Says West Moved 'From Confrontation to Interaction' with Iran," Iranian Labor News Agency, October 30, 2009, IAP20091030950011.

[33] David E. Sanger, Steven Erlanger, and Robert F. Worth, "Iran Rejects Deal to Ship Out Uranium, Officials Report," *The New York Times*, October 30, 2009.

[34] Glenn Kessler and Thomas Erdbrink, "Iran Counters UN on Uranium Plan," *The Washington Post*, October 30, 2009.

[35] Farideh Farhi, "Anatomy of a Nuclear Breakthrough Gone Backwards," *Middle East Report Online*, December 8, 2009, available at <www.merip.org/mero/mero120809.html>.

[36] On October 29, Iranian Ambassador Ali Asghar Soltanieh told IAEA Director General Mohamed ElBaradei that Iran was willing to swap uranium only in batches and to send its low enriched uranium out of the country only when it had the enriched fuel rods for the Tehran Research Reactor (TRR) already in hand. See Sanger, Erlanger, and Worth; and Kessler and Erdbrink. Several weeks later, Foreign Minister Manouchehr Mottaki asserted that any swap would have to take place on Iranian soil. "We will definitely not send our 3.5-percent-enriched uranium out of the country." See Michael Slackman, "Minister Says Iran Won't Ship Uranium Abroad," *The New York Times*, November 19, 2009. In December, Mottaki elaborated that Iran was willing to exchange 400 kilograms, not 1,200 kilos, on the Iranian island of Kish in the Persian Gulf; the rest would be exchanged over "several years." See Robert F. Worth, "Iran Avows Willingness to Swap Some Uranium," *The New York Times*, December 13, 2009.

[37] A senior but anonymous European diplomat stated that the TRR issue had "paralyzed the decision-making process in Tehran." According to the diplomat, "It is a battle over who is tougher or who is more anti-American, and we are in a situation so ridiculous that Ahmadinejad is in the middle." See Glenn Kessler, "Iran Holding up Nuclear Deal with Demand for Reactor Fuel, Diplomat Says," *The Washington Post*, November 6, 2009; also Michael Slackman, "Minister Says Iran Won't Ship Uranium Abroad." As Slackman described the situation, "In the opportunistic, factionalized postelection environment, Mr. Ahmadinejad has emerged as a voice of pragmatism on the nuclear issue, in relative terms, while so-called pragmatic conservatives, like Ali Larijani, the speaker of parliament, and even reformers, like Mir Hussein Moussavi, who lost the election to Mr. Ahmadinejad, have opposed an agreement with the West that was under discussion in the fall." See Michael Slackman, "Hard-Line Rise in Iran Alters View in West," *The New York Times*, December 25, 2009.

From the more moderate end of the leadership spectrum, one Web site reported that Mousavi had charged that "The discussions in Geneva were really surprising, and if the promises given [to the West] are realized, then the hard work of thousands of scientists would be ruined." See Kessler and Erdbrink.

From the hardline side, a column in *Keyhan* asserted that Iran's response to the TRR offer was "that it will not give even one milligram of its enriched uranium to be changed into 20 percent enriched uranium by foreigners." Moreover, "America, Europe and Israel, these American cowboys, old British foxes and Zionist child murderers, want to use this ploy to take Iran's uranium and not give it back." See Thomas Erdbrink, "Iran Officials Appear Split On Nuclear Plan, *The Washington Post*, October 27, 2009.

Several weeks later, *Keyhan* wrote in explicit detail about Iran's stance on the TRR. See "*Keyhan's* analytical report on Tehran's probable stance against delayed response by the West," *Keyhan Online*, November 10, 2009, IAP20091112950057. Several months later, *Keyhan's* editor, Hoseyn Shari'atmadari, would explicitly take Ahmadinejad to task for having fallen for this "dangerous trap" and "trick." See Hoseyn Shari'atmadari, "How did you become so sure?" *Keyhan*, February 6, 2010, IAP20100206950086. For now, Supreme Leader Khamenei warned that it would be "naïve and perverted" to negotiate with the United States. See Thomas Erdbrink and William Branigin, "Iran's Khamenei Rejects U.S. Outreach," *The Washington Post,* November 4, 2009.

[38] Both apparently underestimated the political reaction to the fraudulent June 12 elections and elite skepticism over the terms and conditions of the TRR deal. In addition, Ahmadinejad's many enemies, among both reformers and conservatives, were loath to see him take credit for what could have been a breakthrough in negotiations with the P5+1 and subsequent improvement in relations with the United States. In the end, the fierce criticism over the specifics of the deal and the continuing public demonstrations over the June 12 elections forced the Khamenei-Ahmadinejad regime to back away from the TRR deal negotiated in Geneva and Vienna in October. See Farideh Farhi.

[39] Author's meetings in Moscow, May 2010.

[40] IAEA Director General ElBaradei's earlier report to the Board of Governors had disputed Iran's assertion that construction at the site had started in the second half of 2007. There had actually been construction between 2002 and 2004, which then resumed in 2006, when design work had started. The IAEA charged that Iran's failure to notify the IAEA about the Fordow facility was inconsistent with Iran's Safeguard Agreement obligations. Furthermore, it stated that "Iran's explanation about the purpose of the facility and the chronology of its design and construction requires further clarification." See Helene Cooper and William J. Broad, "UN Agency Says Iran Must Freeze Nuclear Project," *The New York Times*, November 28, 2009; IAEA, Board of Governors resolution adopted, "Implementation of the NPT Safeguards Agreement and relevant provisions of Security Council resolutions 1737 (2006), 1747 (2007), 1803 (2008) and 1835 (2008) in the Islamic Republic of Iran," GOV/2009/82, November 27, 2009; and IAEA Board of Governors, report by the director general, "Implementation of the NPT Safeguards Agreement and relevant provisions of Security Council resolutions 1737 (2006), 1747 (2007), 1803 (2008) and 1835 (2008) in the Islamic Republic of Iran," GOV/2009/74, November 16, 2009.

[41] Thomas Erdbrink, "Iran Vows to Expand its Nuclear Program," *The Washington Post*, November 30, 2009.

[42] "Iran: Ahmadinejad Discusses Nuclear, Economic Issues in TV Interview," Vision of the Islamic Republic of Iran Network 1, December 1, 2009, IAP20091204950001.

[43] Nikolay Surkov, "Threat of Traumatizing Sanctions Hangs Over Iran," *Nezavisimaya Gazeta Online*, December 3, 2009, CEP20091203049007.

[44] Dmitri Trenin, "The Modernization of Russia's Foreign Policy. Q&A with Dmitri Trenin,"

Carnegie Endowment for International Peace, August 2, 2010, available at <www.carnegieendowment. org/publications/index.cfm?fa=view&id=41322>.

[45] "Iran Limits Data to Atomic Agency," *The New York Times*, December 5, 2009.

[46] "Iran's Ahmadinejad to Write Letter to UN Asking for WW2 Compensation," Iranian Labor News Agency, December 19, 2009, IAP20091219950023.

[47] Glenn Kessler, "Iranian Plan Will Move Nation Closer to Having Material for Bomb," *The Washington Post,* February 9, 2010.

[48] "FYI—Russian President Comments on Iran Sanctions, US START Talks," Rossiya 24, March 1, 2010, CEP20100301950283. After Dmitriy Medvedev's comments in France, Moscow pundits debated the consequences of the downward spiral in Russia-Iran relations. At one end of the spectrum, Rajab Safarov, who consistently espoused pro-Iran positions, warned of the dangers. Should sanctions topple Iran's theocracy, "it is not ruled out that [the West] may again take up the idea of turning Iran into a nuclear base against Russia." Therefore, "the Russian leadership should once again think about what poses a bigger threat to Russia—a pro-Western Iran or an Iran with a hypothetical nuclear weapon?" The latter, according to Safarov, "will hardly pose a threat to Russia"; see Rajab Safarov, "Iran Warns," *Vecherniy Dushanbe*, March 3, 2010, CEP20100323950108.

Safarov's arguments were quickly rebutted by Vladimir Sazhin, who contended that "For the most part, no Iran is dangerous to Russia, 'even with a hypothetical nuclear weapon.'" Russia was prepared to work with either a secular or theocratic regime in Tehran, but that regime had to recognize international laws, treaties, and rules. Sazhin almost seemed to suggest that Moscow's relations with Tehran might improve if regime change succeeded and Iran became pro-American again. In contrast to current troubled ties, Moscow's relations with the Shah after 1962 had been "correct and good neighborly," argued Sazhin, quoting then Soviet Foreign Minister Andrey Gromyko. The Shah was a "faithful ally" of the United States, but this did not prevent Iran from becoming "one of Russia's main trade-economic partners in the Near and Middle East"; see Vladimir Sazhin, "What Kind of Iran is Advantageous to Russia?" *Vremya Novostey Online*, March 5, 2010, CEP20100305004009.

[49] "Iran Gives Russian Commercial Pilots Two Months to Leave Country," Iranian Labor News Agency, March 6, 2010, IAP20100306950102; and Olga Bolotova and Igor Bakharev, "Iran Closes Skies to Russians," *Gazeta.ru*, March 6, 2010, CEP201003080490015.

[50] "Iran Bans Tupolev-154 Planes," ITAR–TASS, June 21, 2010, CEP20100621950143.

[51] Colum Lynch, "China Signals Shift on Iran Sanctions," *The Washington Post*, March 25, 2010.

[52] "Medvedev Does Not Rule Out Sanctions Against Tehran," Interfax, April 27, 2010, CEP20100427964016.

[53] Remarks in Washington, DC, January 2010.

[54] Ye. V. Dunaeva.

[55] Irina Filatova, "Medvedev Says Iran Faces Last Chance," *Moscow Times*, May 17, 2010.

[56] Thomas Erdbrink, "Iran to Ship Uranium to Turkey in Nuclear Deal," *The Washington Post*, May 18, 2010.

[57] "Medvedev Warns Iran Deal May Not Be Enough," *Moscow Times*, May 18, 2010. The IAEA at the end of May would report Iran's estimated stockpile of low enriched uranium on May 1, 2010, at 2,427 kilograms. This compared to 1,808 kilograms as of November 22, 2009. See IAEA Board of Gov-

ernors, report by the director general, "Implementation of the NPT Safeguards Agreement and relevant provisions of Security Council resolutions 1737 (2006), 1747 (2007), 1803 (2008) and 1835 (2008) in the Islamic Republic of Iran," GOV/2010/28, May 31, 2010.

[58] Glenn Kessler and Colum Lynch, "U.S., Partners Agree to Sanctions on Iran," *The Washington Post*, May 19, 2010.

[59] Author's meetings in Moscow, May 2010.

[60] Islamic Republic News Agency (IRNA), May 23, 2010, IAP20100523950117.

[61] Vision of the Islamic Republic of Iran Kerman Provincial TV, May 26, 2010, IAP20100526950040.

[62] Rossiya 24, June 5, 2010, CEP20100605950042.

[63] Colum Lynch and Glenn Kessler, "UN Sanctions Against Iran Provoke a Divided Response," *The Washington Post*, June 10, 2010; and UNSC Resolution 1929 (2010), adopted by the Security Council at its 6335th meeting, on June 9, 2010, S/RES/1929.

[64] Colum Lynch and Glenn Kessler, "Gains for Moscow in Iran Deal," *The Washington Post*, May 22, 2010; and Peter Baker and David E. Sanger, "U.S. Makes Concessions to Russia for Iran Sanctions," *The New York Times*, May 22, 2010.

[65] "Russia's Interests in Iran Practically Unaffected by UN Sanctions," ITAR–TASS, June 10, 2010, CEP20100610950348; and "Sale of S–300 not covered by UN sanctions—Russian Foreign Ministry," Interfax, June 10, 2010, CEP20100610950191.

[66] Glenn Kessler and Keith B. Richburg, "Russia Halts Sale of Air Defense Missiles to Iran," *The Washington Post,* June 12, 2010. The move also removed a potential irritant before the June 24 Medvedev-Obama summit, announced the same day.

[67] Steven Erlanger, "France: Russia Stresses Iran Pledge," *The New York Times,* June 12, 2010.

[68] "S–300 Missiles Cannot Be Supplied to Iran—Kremlin Source," Interfax, June 11, 2010, CEP20100611964095. At the same time, the Russian Federal Service for Military-Technical Cooperation (FSVTS) put out a statement declaring, "Expert analysis conducted by the FSVTS of the clauses of the UNSC resolution adopted on 9 June 2010 shows that the restrictive measures and requirements contained in them also affect the issue of the supply of S–300 air defense systems to Iran." See "UN sanctions affect S–300 supplies to Iran—Russian federal service," *Interfax–AVN Online*, June 11, 2010, CEP20100611950172. Still, other notables argued that not going ahead with the S–300 transfers would be a judgment call, not mandated by the resolution. "De jure, we have no impediments to selling such armaments to Iran," declared Deputy Prime Minister Sergei Ivanov. It was now a "question of political will whether we do that or not." See "Russia Has Formal Right to Deliver S–300 to Iran—Ivanov," ITAR–TASS, June 11, 2010, CEP20100611950287. Konstantin Kosachev, head of the Duma's International Affairs Committee, argued that while the resolution did not ban defensive systems, going ahead with transfer of the S–300s, "as if nothing had happened, means setting oneself against real partners, violating the spirit [of the resolution]." Kosachev preferred instead that "the spirit" and not "mercantile interests . . . prevail." See "Senior Russian MP opposes S–300 missile supplies to Iran," Interfax, June 11, 2010, CEP20100611950101.

[69] "AFP [Agence France-Presse]: Ahmadinejad on UN Resolution Says President Obama Made 'Big Mistake,'" Hong Kong AFP, June 11, 2010, CPP20100611968210.

[70] Fedor Lukyanov, "For the U.S., the Desire to Show Iran Who Is Boss Is a Question of Prestige," *Slon.ru Online*, June 10 2010, CEP20100611009004.

[71] "Russia's Lavrov says Iran not to join SCO while it is under sanctions," ITAR–TASS, June 11, 2010, CEP20100611950120.

[72] This was against the background of Medvedev's call, in the same speech, for a "paradigm shift" in Russian foreign policy and "special modernization alliances with our main international partners. . . . First and foremost with countries like Germany, France, Italy, the [European Union] as a whole, the United States of America." See "Medvedev Speech to Envoys Notes 'Paradigm Shift in International Relations,'" speech by Russian President Medvedev at a conference with Russian ambassadors and permanent representatives to international organizations in Moscow on July 12, 2010, Russian Federation President Web site, July 12, 2010, CEP20100713009001.

[73] "Speech by Iranian President Mahmud Ahmadinezhad during a closing ceremony of the Iranian Youth Festival in Tehran," Islamic Republic of Iran News Network Television (IRINN), July 23, 2010, IAP20100724950093.

[74] "Transcript of Remarks by Russian Foreign Minister Sergey Lavrov at the MGIMO [Moscow State Institute of International Relations University] of the MFA of Russia, September 1, 2010, 1164-01-09-2010," Ministry of Foreign Affairs of the Russian Federation Web site, September 2, 2010, CEP20100902950230.

[75] A striking commentary in August 2010 in the hardline conservative daily *Keyhan*, closely tied to Khamenei, looked ahead to success in renewed TRR negotiations. It praised the regime for its conduct the previous October, when it said Iran was able to negotiate with the Western powers without having first to suspend Iran's enrichment program. At the same time, the commentary criticized Mousavi, Larijani, Rafsanjani, and others for what it said had been their decision to use the unrest following the presidential elections to undermine Iranian successes in Geneva and Vienna. As it entered new negotiations, the commentary continued, Iran needed to learn from this past experience. There was reason for hope, argued the commentary: Iran still had leverage, including the issue of 20 percent enrichment; America and Europe were disappointed in the Green Movement; and Khamenei had reestablished "unity" on nuclear policy in Tehran. See Majid Bazrafkan, "A question for the opponents of the Vienna agreement," *Keyhan Online*, August 11, 2010, IAP20100811605002.

By August 20, 2010, according to IAEA estimates, Iran had produced 22 kilograms of 20 percent enriched uranium. See IAEA Board of Governors, report by the director general, "Implementation of the NPT Safeguards Agreement and relevant provisions of Security Council resolutions in the Islamic Republic of Iran," GOV/2010/46, September 6, 2010, available at <www.iaea.org/Publications/Documents/Board/2010/gov2010-46.pdf>. The IAEA report estimated that Iran had produced 2,803 kilograms of low enriched uranium since the start of enrichment in February 2007 and August 6, 2010.

Keyhan's reference to Iran's 20 percent enrichment capability as leverage seemed to hint at a willingness to use it as trade material in a negotiation. In Moscow early the next year, this author would hear that Russian experts considered Iran's stock of 20 percent enriched uranium seriously contaminated and poorly suitable for further enrichment to munitions level. See author's meetings in Moscow,

February 2011. If true, this may have explained Iran's seeming willingness to trade it away. In any event, other hints in this direction subsequently popped up in other Iranian sources, including from Ahmadinejad himself, as did hints of interest in Moscow in going for such a deal.

[76] "Iran Likely to Stop N. Enrichment if Supplied with Fuel," Fars News Agency, September 25, 2010, IAP20100925950082.

[77] Aleksandr Reutov, "Iranian Uranium Becoming Richer," *Kommersant Online*, September 8, 2010, CEP20100908008001. Reutov quotes both the high-level source and Lavrov in this same article.

[78] Russian Federation Presidential Edict No. 1154 of September 22, 2010, "On Measures for the Fulfillment of UN Security Council Resolution 1929 of 9 July 2010," available at <www.kremlin.ru>, September 22, 2010, CEP20100922753001.

[79] Ibid.

[80] "Russia to continue selling arms to Iran—source," Interfax, October 29, 2010, CEP20101029950158; "Iran Gets Russian Arms under Contracts Not Subject to Sanctions," *Interfax–AVN Online*, October 29, 2010, CEP20101029950139; and "Russia Implementing Contract to Deliver Krasnopol Precision Projectiles to Iran," *Interfax–AVN Online*, November 18, 2010, CEP20101118950098. For more on this system, see Walter Williams, "Threat Update Krasnopol—A Laser-Guided Projectile for Tube Artillery," Threat Support Directorate, TRADOC DCSINT, Foreign Military Studies Office, Fort Leavenworth, KS, available at <www.lavoiestrategique.com/3.cours/3. Documentations/3.3articles/Articles/Artillerie/Krasnopol.Russian_Laser_guided_projectil.pdf>.

[81] "Russia Supplies Electronic Intelligence Systems to Iran," RIA Novosti, October 25, 2011, CEP20111025950079.

[82] "Russia will not supply S–300 missile systems to Iran—General Staff," ITAR–TASS, September 22, 2010, CEP20100922950088.

[83] "Russian contract for S–300 missile systems for Iran cancelled—official," Interfax, October 7, 2010, CEP20101007950092.

[84] "Russia to repay under 200m dollars to Iran for cancelled S–300 missiles contract," Interfax, October 7, 2010, CEP20101007950193.

[85] A year later, Defense Minister Ahmad Vahidi acknowledged that Iran had gotten its advance payment back from Russia; see "Iran Files Complaint at ICA over Russians' Breach of S–300 Contract," Fars News Agency, September 28, 2011, IAP20110928950071. The complaint filed at the Paris-based International Court of Arbitration over the broken contract was revealed in late August by Iran's ambassador to Moscow, Mahmud Reza Sajjadi, who said it had been filed 6 months earlier; see "Arms Sales Complaint Not to Hurt Ties with Moscow—Iranian Envoy," Interfax, August 26, 2011, CEP20110826950109. Two months later, Iranian Foreign Ministry spokesman Ramin Mehmanparast asserted that the issue "should not have a negative influence on political relations and they are not having it"; see "S–300 Missile System Refusal Not to Hurt Russia Iran Ties—Iran Spokesman," Interfax, October 10, 2011, CEP201110119500460. Lavrov declared practically the same day that "this case should be closed and no longer talked about"; see "FYI—Minister: No Grounds for Iran to Sue Russia over Cancelled Air-Defense Deal," Ministry of Foreign Affairs of the Russian Federation, October 10, 2011, CEP20111010950080.

[86] "Iran Will Not Attack Any State," interview with Iranian ambassador to Russia Seyed Mahmoud Reza Sajjadi, *Gazeta.ru*, October 21, 2010, CEP20101021037002.

[87] "FYI—Iran to Pursue Russian Compensation for S–300 Non-Delivery," Mehr News Agency, October 23, 2010, IAP20101023950030; and "Minister: Decision to Annul S–300 Delivery to Harm Russia's Interests," Fars News Agency, November 12, 2010, IAP20101112950029.

[88] "FYI—Iran: Ahmadinezhad Delivers Address in North Khorasan," IRINN, November 3, 2010, IAP20101103950063.

[89] Author's meetings in Moscow, May 2010.

[90] Author's meetings in Moscow, February and July 2011.

[91] See, for example, Mark N. Katz, who states that Russia has a "significant economic relationship with Iran," in "Russia's New Diplomatic Idea for Iran," United States Institute of Peace, The Iran Primer, July 26, 2011, <http://iranprimer.usip.org/blog/2011/jul/26/russia%E2%80%99s-new-diplomatic-idea-iran>; or Ilan Berman, who asserts that the "strategic relationship . . . between Moscow and Tehran . . . includes vibrant defense and industrial trade," in "Moscow Should Rethink Its Iran Policy," *Moscow Times*, November 23, 2011, CEP20111124964095.

[92] Author's meetings in Moscow, May 2010.

[93] Rajab Safarov.

[94] Vladimir Sazhin.

[95] Author's meetings in Moscow, May 2010.

[96] "Iran Expels Gazprom Neft from Azar Project, Will Replace It with Iranian Consortium," Interfax, October 10, 2011, CEP20111010964123. Gazprom Neft stated that it was not prepared to work on Iran's terms.

[97] Author's meetings in Moscow, May 2010.

[98] "Amerikanskim sanktsiyam nastal svinets," *Kommersant,* September 9, 2011, available at <www.kommersant.ru/doc/1777119/print>.

[99] Roman Asankin, Yelena Kiseleva, and Seda Yegikyan, "Rusal Digging to Iran: Company Wants to Produce Aluminum and Alumina There," *Kommersant Online*, September 22, 2011, CEP20110922046005.

[100] Olga Bolotova, "Nuclear Aid to Iran. Russia Will Build Several More Nuclear Power Station Units in Iran," *Gazeta.ru*, November 10, 2011, CEP20111111004016.

[101] "Russia Not in Talks with Iran on Building New Nuclear Power Units—Official," RIA Novosti, December 19, 2011, CEP20111219950049.

[102] "Bushehr Provincial TV Reports Signing of $1 Billion Iran-Russia Oil Field Deal," Bushehr Vision of the Islamic Republic of Iran Bushehr Provincial TV, December 18, 2011, IAP20111219808001.

[103] Rick Gladstone, "Iran Admits Western Sanctions Are Inflicting Damage," *The New York Times*, December 20, 2011.

[104] "Lukoil Still Interested in Iran—Fedun," Interfax, October 5, 2011, CEP20111005964133.

[105] Author's meetings in Moscow, July 2011. On Germany-Iran business ties, see also Matthias Kuentzel, "The German Iran Connection," *Welt am Sonntag*, November 27, 2011, EUP20111127014006.

[106] Vladimir Skosyrev, "Iran to Overcome UN Sanctions with Help of China. Tehran and Beijing Increasing Economic Exchange and Military Cooperation," *Nezavisimaya Gazeta Online*, July 18, 2011, CEP20110718049010.

[107] Author's meetings in Moscow, February 2011.

[108] V.I. Sazhin, "Iran: aprel' 2011 g. Voyenno-politicheskaya situatsiya," 11–12, available at <www.iimes.ru/rus/stat/2011/06-06-11c.htm>.

[109] N.A. Kozhanov, *Ekonomicheskiye sanktsii protiv Irana: tseli, masshtaby, vozmozhnyye posledstviya vvedeniya* [Economic Sanctions against Iran: Aims, Scale, Possible Consequences of Implementation] (Moscow: Middle East Institute, 2011), 186–189. Indeed, Iran's $500 billion oil windfall over the past 5 years gave rise at least to one elite restaurant offering $280 fixed-priced meals and $250 dishes of ice cream flecked with edible gold; see Thomas Erdbrink, "In Iran, Resentment over Inequality Grows," *The Washington Post*, August 7, 2011.

[110] Author's meetings in Moscow, July 2011.

[111] "Bushehr Nuclear Plan to Be Commissioned in August—Putin," Interfax, June 8, 2010, CEP20100608964072.

[112] The official inauguration took place on September 12, 2011, a week after the plant was connected to the Iranian power grid on September 3. See "Official Launch of Bushehr Nuclear Power Plant," Ministry of Foreign Affairs of the Russian Federation, September 13, 2011, CEP20110913950007; and "Iran's First Nuclear Power Plant Goes into Operation," *The New York Times*, September 5, 2011.

[113] "Ahmadinejad Chief of Staff: Tehran-Moscow Relations Not Strained," Iranian Students News Agency, October 19, 2010, IAP20101019950052.

[114] "Iran Will Not Attack Any State."

[115] "Iran Ambassador Accuses Media of Distorting Statement About Russia," Interfax, October 29, 2010, CEP20101029964017.

[116] "Iran's Relations with Russia More Important Than S–300 Systems—Ambassador," Interfax, November 29, 2010, CEP20101129950225.

[117] "Iran Has Not Taken Any Step against Russia So Far: Ahmadinejad," Iranian Students News Agency, November 29, 2010, IAP20101129950096.

[118] "Iran Will Not Attack Any State."

[119] V.I. Sazhin, "Iran: yanvar'–fevral' 2011 g. Voyenno-politicheshaya situatsiya" [Iran: January–February 2011. Military-political situation], Institut Blizhnego Vostoka, March 28, 2011, available at <www.iimes.ru/rus/stat/2011/28-03-11c.htm>.

[120] "Tehran Moscow Ties Are Very Important for Region," IRNA, January 29, 2011, IAP20110129950061; and "MP Underscores Iran's Importance for Russia's Position in Middle East," Fars News Agency, February 6, 2011, IAP20110206950018. This was the delegation led by Mehdi Sanaei, head of the Iran-Russia Parliamentary Friendship Group.

[121] Author's meetings in Moscow, February 2011.

[122] "Russian Foreign Minister: Russia Will Not Support Further Sanctions Against Iran," Rossiya 24, February 15, 2011, CEP20110215950106.

[123] Author's meetings in Moscow, February 2011.

[124] Edward Cody, "Russia to Aid NATO on Antimissile Network in Europe," *The Washington Post*, November 21, 2010.

[125] Arkadiy Dubnov, "Conversation on Awkward Topics: Dmitriy Medvedev Has Met with Ahmadinejad and other Caspian Neighbors," *Vremya Novostey Online*, November 19, 2010, CEP20101119004005.

[126] "Iran Must Prove Peaceful Nature of Its Nuclear Program—Medvedev," Interfax, November 21, 2010, CEP20101121964011.

[127] "Iran President Talks with Medvedev of Russia on Phone," IRNA, January 17, 2011, IAP20110117950095; "Medvedev, Ahmadinejad Discuss Economic Cooperation, Political Contacts," Interfax, March 14, 2011, CEP20110314964336; and "Iran, Kazakhstan, Russia Presidents Hold Tripartite Consultations," IRNA, June 15, 2011, IAP20110615950041.

[128] "Tehran, Moscow Underline Increasing Cooperation in Oil, Gas Fields," Fars News Agency, April 7, 2011, IAP20110407950040; and "Iran, Russia Discuss Bilateral Energy Ties," *Press TV Online*, June 24, 2011, IAP20110624950001.

[129] "Tehran, Moscow Ink Transportation MOU," Mehr News Agency, August 6, 2011, IAP20110806950064.

[130] "Iran, Russia Sign Agreement on Building Satellites," Fars News Agency, June 13, 2011, IAP20110613950008.

[131] "Iran, Russian Ministers Discuss Ties," *Press TV Online*, June 8, 2011, IAP20110609950003.

[132] "Deputy Foreign Minister Alexei Borodavkin Meets with Iran Central Bank Delegation," Ministry of Foreign Affairs of the Russian Federation, May 19, 2011, CEP20110519950112.

[133] "Russia Asks Iran to Form Anti Drugs Campaign Intelligence Sharing Center," IRNA, June 17, 2011, IAP20110617950032.

[134] "Official Stresses Iran's Key Role in Campaign Against Terrorism, Narcotics," Fars News Agency, April 30, 2011, IAP20110430950041.

[135] "Iran, Russia Stress Stability, Security in Afghanistan," Fars News Agency, April 5, 2011, IAP20110405950056.

[136] "Russian, Iranian Diplomats Discuss Syrian Problem, Interfax, July 1, 2011, CEP20110701964017.

[137] Arkadiy Dubnov.

[138] Author's meetings in Moscow, May 2010 and February 2011.

[139] N.K. Ter-Oganov, "Iran: vlast' I oppozitsiya" [Iran: power and opposition], Near East Institute, February 13, 2011, available at <www.iimes.ru/rus/stat/2011/13-02-11a.htm>; Neil MacFarquhar, "Mystery Deepens on Status of Iran Opposition Leaders," *The New York Times*, March 1, 2011; and Alan Cowell, "Hard-Liners Ruling Iran Gain Ally in Key Post," *The New York Times*, March 9, 2011.

[140] By early summer 2011, they succeeded in forcing three embarrassing course reversals on Ahmadinejad after attracting Khamenei to their side. The Supreme Leader overruled the president when the latter on April 16 tried to fire Intelligence Minister Heydar Moslehi, after which the president disappeared for 1 day. The next month, the Guardian Council reversed Ahmadinejad's firing of three cabinet ministers. Then in June, Ahmadinejad was forced to give up on his attempt personally to take over the Oil Ministry. See Mehdi Khalaji, "Iran's Continuing Power Struggles," PolicyWatch #1799, The Washington Institute for Near East Policy, April 20, 2011, available at <www.washingtoninstitute. org/print.php?template=C05&CID=3352>; Robert Tait, "Ahmadinejad Floored by Bugs, Spirits, and Djinns," Radio Free Europe/Radio Liberty, May 6, 2011, available at <www.rferl.org/articleprint-view/24093844.html>; Clifford Krauss, "Ahmadinejad Backs Out of Key Role at OPEC," *The New York Times*, May 25, 2011; and "Iran: President Yields on Oil Ministry," *The New York Times*, June 3, 2011.

A common target in many of the attacks on Ahmadinejad was his chief of staff, Esfandiar Rahim Mashaei. His daughter was married to the president's son and it was widely thought that the president was grooming Mashaei to succeed him. Clerics and conservative critics objected to the two men's playing up of pre-Islamic Iranian civilization and the imminent reappearance of the "Hidden Imam." See Khalaji; and Thomas Erdbrink, "Arrests Suggest Rift in Iran's Leadership," *The Washington Post*, May 7, 2011. In October 2010, as some in Tehran sought to temper the reaction to Moscow's cancellation of the S–300 contract, Mashaei had asserted that Russian-Iranian relations were not "strained." See "Ahmadinejad Chief of Staff: Tehran-Moscow Relations Not Strained," Iranian Students News Agency, October 19, 2010, IAP20101019950052.

But it was also Mashaei who reportedly tried repeatedly to reach out to Washington in spring 2011 to open a dialogue. See David Ignatius, "Overtures and Anger in Tehran," *The Washington Post*, May 6, 2011. In 2008, Mashaei also appeared to reach out to Israel, but had to back off by the end of the year; see Dudi Cohen, "Iranian VP: We are friends of the nation in Israel," YNet News, July 19, 2008, available at <www.ynetnews.com/Ext/Comp/ArticleLayout/CdaArticlePrintPreview/1,2506,L-3570266,00.html>; and Dudi Cohen, "Iranian VP calls for Israel's destruction," YNet News, December 9, 2008, available at <www.ynetnews.com/ExtCom/ArticleLayout/CdaArticlePrintPreview/1,2506,L-3636063,00.html>. In Moscow, the word was that Mashaei had been cut off at the knees for this initiative; see author's meetings in Moscow, July 2011.

As the anti-Ahmadinejad campaign gathered steam in Tehran in late spring 2011, critics charged that the president had been "bewitched" by his advisor and called for Mashaei's arrest. See Thomas Erdbrink, "Ayatollah: Iran's President 'Bewitched' by Senior Aide," *The Washington Post*, May 16, 2011; and Associated Press, "Iran: Publication Calls for Arrest of President's Closest Political Aide," *The Washington Post*, May 19, 2011.

[141] Author's meetings in Moscow, February and July 2011.

[142] "Iran Praises Russian Plan to Restart Nuclear Talks," *The New York Times*, August 17, 2011.

[143] David E. Sanger, "Easing Stance, Iran Offers Inspectors 'Supervision' of Nuclear Program," *The New York Times*, September 6, 2011.

[144] This most recently centered on an alleged $2.6 billion bank fraud involving Ahmadinejad's chief of staff Mashaei and on Ali Khamenei's suggestion to abolish the presidency. See Thomas Erdbrink, "High-level Iranian Banker Flees Amid Scandal," *The Washington Post*, September 29, 2011; David D. Kirkpatrick, "In Rebuke to Iran's President, Courts Void Release of Hikers," *The New York Times*, September 15, 2011; Thomas Erdbrink, "In Iran, a New Challenge to Hard-liners," *The Washington Post*, October 21, 2011; and Robert F. Worth, "Iran's Power Struggle Goes Beyond Personalities to Future of Presidency Itself," *The New York Times*, October 27, 2011.

[145] Seyyed Yahya Hoseyni, "The Step-by-Step Proposal, A New Test for Moscow," *Payam-e Ostan-e*, September 12, 2011, IAP20110914808001.

[146] *Persian Dreams*, 253.

[147] Author's meetings in Moscow, February and July 2011.

[148] Author's meetings in Moscow, July 2011.

[149] Author's meetings in Moscow, May 2010.

[150] Author's meetings in Moscow, July 2011.

[151] "Iran, Kazakhstan, Russia Presidents Hold Tripartite Consultations," IRNA, June 15, 2011, IAP20110615950041; and "Medvedev, Ahmadinejad Discussed More Constructive Interaction of Iran and Sextet—Lavrov," Interfax, June 15, 2011, CEP20110615964183. As pointed out earlier, the bilateral meeting in Yekaterinburg in 2009, right after Ahmadinejad's contested reelection, had provoked "Death to Russia" chants at Green Movement demonstrations in Tehran. Ahmadinejad skipped the 2010 SCO summit in Tashkent, which took place just after Russia and China had supported Resolution 1929 in the UNSC.

[152] "Moscow, Tehran Starting on Fresh Page in Relations—Iranian Foreign Minister," Interfax, August 17, 2011, CEP20110817964064.

[153] "Russian Foreign Ministry Condemns IAEA Report on Iran," Ministry of Foreign Affairs of the Russian Federation, November 9, 2011, CEP20111109950182. This was in reference to IAEA Board of Governors, report by the director general, "Implementation of the NPT Safeguards Agreement and relevant provisions of Security Council resolutions in the Islamic Republic of Iran," GOV/2011/65, November 8, 2011.

[154] "Medvedev Speech to Envoys Notes 'Paradigm Shift in International Relations.'"

[155] "Russian Defense Ministry Plans to Upgrade Qabala Radar Given Iranian Missile Program—Serdyukov (Part 2)," Interfax, November 18, 2011, CEP20111118964035.

[156] Ivan Safronov, Jr., "General Staff Prepares for War and Acknowledges the Military-Industrial Complex's Lack of Preparedness for It," *Kommersant Online*, November 18, 2011, CEP20111118037001.

[157] Author's meetings in Moscow, May 2010, and February and July 2011.

[158] Ibid.

[159] Victoria Kupchinetskaya interview of Vladimir Sazhin and National Defense University's Michael Kofman, Voice of America panel discussion, "Kto boitsya Iranskogo atoma?" November 17, 2011, available at <www.youtube.com/watch?v=VRZ_IGi46e4>.

[160] Author's meetings in Moscow, July 2011. Olli Heinonen, former deputy director of the IAEA, recently stated that in his opinion Iran will reach the "break-out capability," which he defined as "the capacity to produce weapons-grade uranium," by the end of 2012; see *Spiegel* interview with former nuclear watchdog, "The Iranians 'Tricked and Misled Us,'" *Spiegel Online*, October 6, 2011, available at <www.spiegel.de/international/world/0,1518,druck-790042,00.html>.

[161] Author's meetings in Moscow, May 2010, and February and July 2011.

[162] Author's meetings in Moscow, May 2010 and February 2011.

[163] Vladimir Yevseyev, "The Iranian Nuclear Arsenal: Foggy Uncertainty," *Nezavisimoye Voyennoye Obozreniye*, September 30, 2011, available at <http://nvo.ng.ru/armament/2011-09-30/8_iran.html>.

[164] Antonov in Ekho Moskvy radio interview as reported in "Russian deputy defense minister says Russia, NATO differ on Iran missile threat," *Interfax–AVN Online*, June 11, 2011, CEP20110611950042.

[165] Author's meetings in Moscow, February 2011.

[166] Vladimir Yevseyev, "A Real Path to Joint Missile Defense," *New Eastern Outlook*, April 27, 2011, available at <http://journal-neo.com/?q=print/6116>; Major-General (Ret.) Vladimir Dvorkin, "There Will Be Either a Joint Missile Defense, or . . . ," *Voyenno-Promyshlennyy Kuryer Online*, February 9, 2011, CEP20110405351001; and Dvorkin, "The Time Has Come to Forget about Threats of a European Missile Defense: Obstacles in the Path of Cooperation of Russia and the West Do Not Involve Military Security," *Nezavisimoye Voyennoye Obozreniye Online*, September 30, 2011, CEP20111012381001.

[167] Author's meetings in Moscow, May 2010, and February and July 2011.

[168] *Persian Dreams*, passim.

[169] The Levada Institute polled 1,600 people 18 years and older living in 130 communities spread across 45 regions of the Russian Federation; see <www.levada.ru/press/2011060103.html>.

[170] Levada polling in February–March 2010 as reported in "Opinion Poll: Russian Attitudes towards the 'Iranian Threat,'" *Russian Analytical Digest*, no. 83, September 28, 2010, 11–12, drawing on <www.levada.ru/press/2010032606.html>, and <www.levada.ru/press/2009063005.html>, which deals with Russian assistance to Iran.

[171] Author's meetings in Moscow, May 2010, and February and July 2011.

[172] Author's meetings in Moscow, May 2010.

[173] Author's meetings in Moscow, May 2010, and February and July 2011.

[174] On Iran's involvement in Tajikistan in 1992, see *Persian Dreams*, 57–102.

[175] Author's meetings in Moscow, May 2010, and February and July 2011.

[176] Author's meetings in Moscow, May 2010. On Iran's so-called restraint in the Caucasus, see also Vladimir Sazhin, who points out that extremists in this region are Wahabis who consider Iranian Shi'ites to be heretics.

[177] Author's meetings in Moscow, July 2011.

[178] See, for example, Dmitri Trenin and Alexey Malashenko, "Iran: A View from Moscow," Carnegie Endowment for International Peace, Washington, DC, 2010. For recent discussions of Iran's pragmatic approach to the Caucasus and Central Asia, see Farhad Atai, "The Dynamics of Bilateral Relations in the South Caucasus: Iran and Its North Neighbors," *China and Eurasia Forum Quarterly* 7, no. 3 (November 2009), 115–128; Haley Sweetland Edwards, "Iran's New Abroad: Beset by Global Sanctions, Iran's Leaders Go Local," *Foreign Policy*, September 20, 2010; and Sebastien Peyrouse and Sadykzhan Ibraimov, "Iran's Central Asia Temptations," *Current Trends in Islamist Ideology* 10, Center on Islam, Democracy and the Future of the Muslim World, August 17, 2010.

[179] *Persian Dreams*, 288–289.

[180] Ibid., 289. All the same time, there has been speculation over the years alleging ties between Iranian surrogate Hizballah and Chechen militants.

[181] Grigoriy Sanin, "The Hunt for Beznogiy (Legless)," *Itogi*, July 11, 2011, CEP20110718546001.

[182] *Persian Dreams*, 288–290.

[183] Ibid., 301–306.

[184] Author's meetings in Moscow, February 2011.

[185] See *Persian Dreams*, 150–153, 156–159, and 162–164.

[186] "Russia gets ready for the Caspian Sea war," *Segonya.ru*, May 10, 2011, CEP20110512358001.

[187] Yaroslav Vyatkin, "Russia Successfully Beat Back an Iranian Attack," *Argumenty Nedeli Online*, October 5, 2011, CEP20111006358006; Yuliya Zimakova, "An Excellent Result for Each Exercise Day!" *Kaspiyets*, October 7, 2011, CEP20111011358005; and Aleksandr Khramchikhin, "Exercises: 'Tsentr' Approached the Outskirts: The Russian Army Together with Its CSTO Allies Has Conducted an Anti-Extremist Exercise," *Nezavisimoye Voyennoye Obozreniye Online*, October 7, 2011, CEP20111007358014.

[188] Author's meetings in Moscow, February 2011.

[189] Colum Lynch, "Russia and China Block Syria Resolution at UN," *The Washington Post*, October 5, 2011.

[190] Thomas Erdbrink and Joby Warrick, "Iran Fears the Worst as West Steps Up Pressure," *The Washington Post*, January 6, 2012.

[191] Author's meetings in Moscow, May 2010, and February and July 2011.

[192] A.A. Dynkin and V.G. Baranovskiy, *Rossiya i Mir: 2011. Ekonomika i Vneshnyaya Politika. Yezhegodnyi Prognos* [Russia and the World: 2011. Economy and Foreign Policy. Annual Forecast] (Moscow: IMEMO, 2010), 129. See also A.A. Dynkin, ed., *Strategicheskiy global'nyy prognoz 2030* [Strategic Global Forecast 2030] (Moscow: IMEMO, 2011), 67, 70.

[193] Author's meetings in Moscow, May 2010.

[194] Dvorkin, "There Will Be Either a Joint Missile Defense, or . . . ."

[195] "'Nuclear Club' Expansion May Drag Russia into Military Conflicts—RVSN Commander (Part 2)," Interfax, December 16, 2011, CEP20111216964171.

[196] Author's meetings in Moscow, May 2010.

[197] Author's meetings in Moscow, July 2011.

[198] *Persian Dreams*, 117. Russia withdrew from the agreement effective December 1, 2000, early in Putin's first term as president; see *Persian Dreams*, 142–143.

[199] Peter Baker and Susan Glasser, *Kremlin Rising: Vladimir Putin's Russia and the End of Revolution* (New York: Scribner, 2005), 122–123, 129–134; and *Persian Dreams*, 186–187.

[200] "Putin at the Munich Conference on Security Policy, Germany, February 10, 2007," Ministry of Foreign Affairs (Internet Version-WWW), February 12, 2007, CEP20070212950109.

[201] *Persian Dreams*, 247–274, 289–292, 301–310.

[202] Author's meetings in Moscow, May 2010 and July 2011.

[203] "Russia, China Pressuring IAEA on Iran: Diplomats," Agence France-Presse, October 25, 2011, EUP20111025085023; "Comment by the Russian Ministry of Foreign Affairs information and press department on a media question about an IAEA report on a possible nuclear dimension to Iran's nuclear programme," Ministry of Foreign Affairs of the Russian Federation, October 25, 2011, CEP20111025950197; "Russia: Foreign Minister Supports UN Sanctions Against Iran, Criticizes 'Unilateral' Ones," Ekho Moskvy Radio, October 21, 2011, CEP20111021950170.

[204] "Russia: Foreign Minister Supports UN Sanctions Against Iran, Criticizes 'Unilateral' Ones."

[205] "Medvedev Does Not Rule Out Sanctions Against Tehran."

[206] *Persian Dreams*, 296–299 and 310.

[207] Author's meetings in Moscow, May 2010; and Vladimir Sazhin.

[208] *Persian Dreams*, 1–5.

[209] Joby Warrick, "Iran 'Set Back' on Nuclear Program," *The Washington Post*, October 18, 2011.

[210] Jerry Markon and Karen DeYoung, "U.S. Says Iran Plotted to Kill Saudi Envoy," *The Washington Post*, October 12, 2011; and Helene Cooper, "Obama Says Facts Support Accusation of Iranian Plot," *The New York Times*, October 14, 2011.

[211] Isabel Kershner, "Israel Tests a Long-Range Missile," *The New York Times*, November 3, 2011; Isabel Kershner and David E. Sanger, "Israel Faces Questions About News Reports of Eyeing Iran Strike," *The New York Times*, November 4, 2011; and Joel Greenberg, "In Israel, Speculation about Strike on Iran," *The Washington Post*, November 4, 2011.

[212] David E. Sanger and Mark Landler, "To Isolate Iran, U.S. Presses UN on Nuclear Data," *The New York Times*, October 16, 2011.

[213] "Implementation of the NPT Safeguards Agreement and relevant provisions of Security Council resolutions in the Islamic Republic of Iran," IAEA Board of Governors, report by director general, GOV/2011/65, November 8, 2011.

[214] Robert F. Worth and Artin Afkhami, "High Emotion and Intrigue after Iran Blast," *The New York Times*, November 15, 2011; and William J. Broad, "Images Show Devastation at Iran Base After Blast," *The New York Times*, November 30, 2011. The explosion occurred on November 12.

[215] IAEA Board of Governors, resolution adopted on November 18, 2011, "Implementation of the NPT Safeguards Agreement and relevant provision of the United Nations Security Council resolutions in the Islamic Republic of Iran," GOV/2011/69, November 18, 2011.

[216] Joby Warrick, "U.S., Allies Hit Iran with New Sanctions over Nuclear Efforts," *The Washington Post*, November 22, 2011.

[217] Thomas Erdbrink and Joby Warrick, "Iranians Attack British Embassy," *The Washington Post*, November 30, 2011; and Thomas Erdbrink and Joby Warrick, "Iran Facing Increased Isolation after Embassy Rampage," *The Washington Post*, December 1, 2011.

[218] Edward Cody and Thomas Erdbrink, "European Nations Bolster Sanctions Against Iran," *The Washington Post*, December 2, 2011; and Rick Gladstone and Nicholas Kulish, "West Tightens Iran Sanctions After Embassy Attack," *The New York Times*, December 2, 2011.

[219] The Foreign Ministry put out a statement asserting that Moscow was "ready to cooperate with all interested states, including the United States." See "Russia concerned by reports on planned terror attacks in USA—ministry," Ministry of Foreign Affairs of the Russian Federation, October 12, 2011, CEP20111012950208. Lavrov cautioned that Moscow would not comment on the alleged conspiracy until after hearing American experts lay out the case; see "Russia Not to Comment on Alleged Iran Murder Plot Before U.S. Explanations—Lavrov," Interfax, October 18, 2011, CEP20111018964016.

[220] The statement said that Russia was "very concerned that the report is already being used with a vengeance to undermine the international community's efforts to bring about a political and diplomatic settlement of the situation regarding the Iranian nuclear program as soon as possible. The future sequence of events may turn down a dangerous and confrontational path. We also see an attempt to deal a blow to Russian initiatives, the aim of which is to assist in resolving the problem on a gradual and mutual basis"; see "Comment from the information and press department at the Russian Foreign Ministry on IAEA Director-General Y. Amano's new report on 8 November on the Iranian nuclear program," Ministry of Foreign Affairs of the Russian Federation, November 9, 2011, CEP20111109950182.

[221] Nikolay Pakhomov, "The IAEA Report: Without Sensations and Consequences," *Politkom. ru*, November 11, 2011, CEP20111111004017.

[222] "Russian Pundits Comment on IAEA Report on Iran's Nuclear Program," RIA Novosti, November 9, 2011, CEP20111109950158.

[223] IAEA Board of Governors, resolution adopted on November 18, 2011; and "Statement by the Russian Foreign Ministry in connection with the adoption of a resolution on the Iranian nuclear

program by the IAEA Board of Governors," Ministry of Foreign Affairs of the Russian Federation, November 18, 2011, CEP20111118950164.

[224] "Moscow Condemns Attack on UK Embassy in Iran," Interfax, November 30, 2011, CEP20111130964015.

[225] "Russia Calls New U.S. Sanctions on Iran Unacceptable," *Moscow Times Online*, November 23, 2011, CEP20111123964111; and Bradenstein interview with Ryabkov, "Any Act of Terror is Unjustified."

[226] "Russia in New Criticism of Iran Sanctions, UN Nuclear Agency Report," Rossiya 24, December 1, 2011, CEP20111201950144.

[227] "Iran, Russia Sign Agreement on 'Strategic Cooperation,'" IRNA, November 11, 2011, IAP20111111950021.

[228] "Larijani: Iran Russia Relations Growing," IRNA, November 29, 2011, IAP20111129950135.

[229] Will Englund, "Putin Pulls in a Wave of Boos on Fight Night," *The Washington Post*, November 22, 2011.

[230] Gregory L. White and Rob Barry, "Russia's Dubious Vote," *The Wall Street Journal*, December 28, 2011, available at <http://online.wsj.com/article/SB10001424052970203391104577124540544822220.html#>.

[231] "Putin Ally Quits as Speaker of Parliament," *The Washington Post*, December 15, 2011; Ellen Barry, "On TV, Putin Is Dismissive of Critics Far and Near," *The New York Times*, December 16, 2011; and Michael Birnbaum, "Medvedev Urges Political Reforms in Russia," *The Washington Post*, December 23, 2011.

[232] Ellen Barry and Michael Schwirtz, "Putin's Opponents Hold Vast Rally, Promising More," *The New York Times*, December 25, 2011; "Reiting Putina snizilsya, no eshchyo dostatochen dlya pobedy v pervom ture," available at <www.newsru.com/russia/29dec2011/putinrate.html>; "Poll Shows Slight Increase in Russian Leaders' Approval Ratings," Interfax, December 30, 2011, CEP20111230950123.

[233] "Russian protest leader outlines his short-term strategy," *LiveJournal*, December 27, 2011, CEP20111229950180.

[234] Author's meetings in Moscow, February and July 2011.

[235] Hamed Khabiri, "Coup by the Circle of Medvedev in Russia's Foreign Policy," *Javan Online*, June 1, 2010, IAP20100602744002. The document in question had been drafted in February 2010, but did not appear in public until mid-May 2010. See "Apparent Text of 'Leaked' Draft of Russian Foreign Policy Document [Program for the Effective Systemic Utilization of Foreign Policy Factors in Support of the Long-Term Development of the Russian Federation] and Accompanying Letter to President Medvedev from Foreign Minister S. Lavrov [dated February 10, 2010]," *Russkiy Newsweek Online*, May 11, 2010, CEP20100514037004. In fact, the document's passages on Iran were all relatively plain.

[236] Erlanger.

[237] "Russia Has No Grounds to Suspect Iran of Seeking to Possess Nuclear Weapons—Putin," Interfax, December 2, 2010, CEP20101202964015.

[238] See "Medvedev Speech to Envoys Notes 'Paradigm Shift in International Relations.'"

[239] "Russian President Dmitriy Medvedev's statement regarding the situation surrounding Iran," September 25, 2009, CEP20090925950288.

[240] Aleksandr Artemyev, Sergey Smirnov, and Yekaterina Vinokurova, "Reset of Reset," *Gazeta.ru*, October 3, 2011, CEP20111004557003.

[241] Author's meetings in Moscow, July 2011.

[242] See, for example, Andrew E. Kramer, "Economic Reforms Likely to Continue Under Putin," *The New York Times*, September 25, 2011; and Aleksey Venediktov, "Putin—sovetskiy ofitser Brezhnevskoy epokhi," available at <www.echo.msk.ru/blog/pressa_echo/776775-echo/>.

[243] "Russian Industry Up 6.5%, Prices 0.1% in July—Analysts," Interfax, August 1, 2011, CEP20110801964173; "Russia's GDP to Grow 2%–2.5% with Oil at $80 per Barrel, or Decrease by 1.5%–2% at $60—Nabiullina," Interfax, October 6, 2011, CEP20111006964105; and "Citi Reduces Russia's GDP Growth Forecast for 2012 to 2.5%," Interfax, September 30, 2011, CEP20110930964151.

[244] On all the issues in this paragraph and the next, see also John W. Parker, *Russia's Revival: Ambitions, Limitations, and Opportunities for the United States*, INSS Strategic Perspectives, No. 3 (Washington, DC: NDU Press, January 2011), 3–17, 22.

[245] "Russia's acting finance minister concerned about capital flight," Rossiya 24, December 5, 2011, CEP20111205950243; and "Net Capital Outflow from Russia in Nine Months of 2011 amounts to 49.3bn Dollars," Interfax, October 4, 2011, CEP20111004950173.

[246] Seth Mydans, "Putin's Eye for Power Leads Some in Russia to Ponder Life Abroad," *The New York Times*, October 2, 2011. See also "Young Russians Want to Emigrate in Search of Better Living Standards—Poll," Interfax, September 28, 2011, CEP20110928950099.

[247] "Russia Faces Demographic Decline—Security Chief," Interfax, September 13, 2011, CEP20110913950055. See also Ivan Yegorov, "Island Seeks Engineer," *Rossiyskaya Gazeta Online*, September 14, 2011, CEP20110914557004. Patrushev's projection implicitly contradicted Putin's endorsement in 2007 of a "Concept of Demographic Policy to 2025," which foresaw a rise in overall population to 145 million by 2025. See Parker, *Russia's Revival*, 11.

[248] "Sacked Minister Reiterates Cause of His 'Conflict' with Russian President," Interfax, October 10, 2011, CEP20111010950062.

[249] Diane Cardwell and Rick Gladstone, "Oil Prices Predicted to Stay above $100 a Barrel Through Next Year," *The New York Times*, December 29, 2011.

[250] Denis Sinyakov, Reuters, "Kudrin Sees Threat from Pensions and Oil," *Moscow Times Online*, September 14, 2011, CEP20110914964051.

[251] Ruslan Pukhov, "The Real Cost of Modernizing the Military," *Moscow Times Online*, October 6, 2011, CEP20111006964276.

[252] Will Englund, "Putin Warns of 'Bitter Pills' for Russian Economy," *The New York Times*, September 24, 2011.

[253] See, for example, Aleksey Venediktov, "Putin—sovetskiy ofitser Brezhnevskoy epokhi," available at <www.echo.msk.ru/blog/pressa_echo/776775-echo/>; and Kramer. On Putin's record during his first two terms as president, See Parker, *Russia's Revival*, 5–8.

[254] Yevgeniya Pismennaya, "Putinu predlozheny neudobnyye dlya nego reformy," *Vedomosti.ru*, December 30, 2011, available at <www.vedomosti.ru/politics/news/1467117/programma_peremen#ixzz1i0G4kkNV>.

[255] Sergey Smirnov and Yelizaveta Surnacheva, "They Have Missed Obama: The Kremlin Has Sent Barack Obama a Special Invitation to Visit Moscow on 13 December," *Gazeta.ru*, October 31, 2011, CEP20111101009010. See also "Russian, U.S. negotiators Discuss Missile Defence," Ministry of Foreign

Affairs of the Russian Federation, October 16, 2011, CEP20111016950037; and "Moscow Preparing 'Low-cost', but 'Effective' Response to U.S. Missile Defense in Europe—Newspaper," Interfax, October 14, 2011, CEP20111014964020.

[256] Will Englund, "Russia Threatens to Target U.S. Missile Shield," *The Washington Post*, November 24, 2011; and "Russia's Response to Creation of U.S. Missile Defense System in Europe Won't Make Negotiation Impossible—Medvedev," Interfax, November 21, 2011, CEP20111121964150.

[257] "New Russian President to Decide on Attending NATO Summit in Chicago—Envoy," RIA Novosti, October 3, 2011, CEP20111003950079.

[258] In addition, it may be that well-reasoned critiques of the Russian position on missile defense, offered by experts such as Dvorkin, have found readers at the top in Moscow. See Dvorkin, "There Will Be Either a Joint Missile Defense, or . . ."; and Dvorkin, "The Time Has Come to Forget about Threats of a European Missile Defense"; and Vladimir Yevseyev, "A Real Path to Joint Missile Defense," *New Eastern Outlook*, April 27, 2011, available at <http://journal-neo.com/?q=print/6116>.

[259] For a good recent summary, see "Strike the Iron While Obama Is in Office," *Moscow Times Online*, October 14, 2011, CEP20111014964155.

[260] Natalya Kostenko, "Rokirovka vo vlasti polozhila konets modernizatsii," *Vedomosti.ru*, December 30, 2011, available at <www.vedomosti.ru/politics/news/1467118/vse_dlya_fronta#ixzz1iOH0yaF>.

[261] Although Russia's accession to the World Trade Organization is now a done deal, followup debate in the U.S. Congress over repeal of the Jackson-Vanik amendment and granting Russia permanent normal trade relations with the United States promises to be contentious and will spark a Russian reaction. However, Moscow most likely will not want to upset the applecart of "reset" and will keep its reaction fairly muted.

[262] Colum Lynch, "Russia and China Block Syria Resolution at UN," *The Washington Post*, October 5, 2011; and "Russian president speaks about Syria at Security Council meeting—text," UNSC, October 7, 2011, CEP20111007950169.

[263] Yevgeniy Shestakov, "Russia Stops a New War. Moscow Did Not Support the 'Libyan Scenario' with Regard to Syria," *Rossiyskaya Gazeta Online*, October 6, 2011, CEP20111006049002.

About the Author

John W. Parker is a Senior Research Fellow in the Center for Strategic Research, Institute for National Strategic Studies, at the National Defense University. He served previously in the U.S. Department of State's Bureau of Intelligence and Research, where he was Deputy Office Director and Chief of the Division for Caucasus and Central Asia in the Office for Russian and Eurasian Analysis. His principal areas of expertise are Russia and the states of the former Soviet Union and Russian-Iranian relations. He has served two tours at the American Embassy in Moscow, where he was Chief of the Political/Internal Section from 1989 to 1991, and was Deputy Director of the U.S. Information Agency's "Research and Development—USA" exhibit in the Soviet Union in 1972. Dr. Parker has also been a Public Policy Scholar at the Woodrow Wilson International Center for Scholars and a Guest Scholar at the Brookings Institution. He holds a Bachelor of Arts degree from Indiana University and a Ph.D. from Yale University.